SOLDIER F: SAS

GUERRILLAS IN THE JUNGLE

D1146744

TITLES IN SERIES FROM 22 BOOKS

continued at back of book . . .

SOLDIER F: SAS

GUERRILLAS IN THE JUNGLE

Shaun Clarke

First published in Great Britain 1993
22 Books, 3 Sheldon Way, Larkfield, Maidstone, Kent

Copyright © 1993 by 22 Books

The moral right of the author has been asserted

A CIP catalogue record for this book is available from the
British Library

ISBN 1 898125 07 4

10 9 8 7 6 5 4 3 2

Printed and bound in Great Britain by
Caledonian International Book Manufacturing Ltd, Glasgow

Prelude

The guerrilla camp had been hacked out of the dense jungle and could be seen only from the air. Its centrepiece was a roughly levelled parade ground, about the size of a tennis court, though such a game was unknown to these people. Built in the natural caverns of red and ochre rock camouflaged by the overhanging foliage, the camp quarters consisted of a lean-to thatched with *atap* palm, with kitchen, lecture room, and sleeping benches for about sixty newcomers. The older hands were housed in an *atap* further up the hill, above the boulder and overlooking the parade ground.

A babbling stream, providing water for the camp, snaked around the boulder, past the parade ground and back into the dense, steaming jungle. The latrines were built further away, near to where the stream entered the jungle, carrying the excrement and urine to the isolated dwellings that used the same water for washing and drinking. The latrines themselves consisted of a thatched lean-to over a pit full of seething maggots. The stench was atrocious.

Few of the guerrillas were more than twenty-five years of age, most were under twenty, and a surprising number were little more than children. Some of the males wore khaki shorts, shirts and military caps, but most wore no item of uniform and were either dressed like coolies or wearing white shirts, grey trousers and felt hats. Most of them were barefoot, though some wore *terumpas* – wooden clogs held on by rubber straps.

Almost without exception, the women were in long-sleeved, high-necked white smocks and wide black trousers. All had bobbed hair and used no make-up. The better-educated taught Mandarin and singing; the others worked in the kitchen and did their fair share of the dirtiest, heaviest male chores. Though all of them acted as nurses, seamstresses and general domestics, they expected to be treated just like the men and could be just as merciless when it came to the treatment of prisoners or traitors.

The daily schedule was strict and demanding. Reveille was at first light, 5.30 in the morning, when the crying of gibbons and the clicking of cicadas dominated the chatter of the jungle. At 6.00, when the guerrillas had bathed and brushed their teeth, they took part in the flag-raising ceremony, singing 'The Red Flag'. Roll-call was followed by a communal reading of the laws and regulations of the Malayan Races' Liberation Army (MRLA). Calisthenics lasted until 6.30, followed by a cup of tea and a rest period.

At 7.00 they started drilling with weapons. This included practice in jungle-warfare tactics, racing up and down hills, climbing trees and learning various jungle ambush positions. At 8.30 they washed and rested, then had a breakfast of boiled tapioca or rice with greens – fern tops or sweet-potato leaves – followed by a second rest period.

Classes began at 10.00 sharp, with political and military lessons on a daily alternating basis, the former covering Marxism–Leninism, the writings of Mao Tse-tung and the current international situation; the latter, map-reading, tactical theory, lessons in the tactics of the Russian and Chinese armies, and the general principles of guerrilla warfare.

Depending on the length of the lectures, these classes would last until approximately noon, when the guerrillas would break for a snack of biscuits and hot water, with a rest period lasting until 1.00 p.m. From then until 3.00 they would have individual assignments: special instruction in Mandarin or general study groups for the new recruits; preparation for the next lectures by the instructors; jobs around the camp – collecting firewood, cleaning up, ministering to the many sick – then, at 3.00, another arduous hour of drilling with weapons. This was followed by a thirty-minute wash period and, at 4.30, the 'evening' meal, not much different from breakfast.

Even during the so-called 'free period' lasting until 6.00, they would be compelled to study or practice their drills.

At 6.00, after coffee, there was a parade of all hands to take down the colours and sing 'The Red Flag' again. Then the 'political research' would begin, with experienced political warriors leading group discussions about the doctrines of Communism. These discussions would include 'self-criticism' and 'mutual criticism' designed to eradicate the ego. No one smiled. Jokes were rarely made. Throughout every activity, they would repeatedly give one another the clenched-fist salute.

When the discussions ended, at 9.00 p.m. sharp, they went straight to bed.

Given such a harsh, undeviating routine, to be called upon to join a patrol into the jungle often seemed like a blessing.

*   *   *

GUERRILLAS IN THE JUNGLE

All of the men and women in that particular morning's patrol were Chinese Malays. While some had been born in Malaya, others in China and a few in Hong Kong, Borneo or Sumatra, they all spoke Kuo-yü, the national dialect of China and the lingua franca of the jungle. They spoke in a whisper, and then only for the first few minutes; once away from the camp, deep in the jungle, they maintained a resolute silence, communicating only with hand signals.

Their armament for the patrol consisted of a British Bren gun, three antiquated tommy-guns, ten rifles, five shotguns, five pistols and a *parang*, or Malay jungle knife, shaped like a machete, one of which was carried by each member of the patrol.

From the vegetable gardens and rubber trees at the edge of the camp, they plunged straight into the darkness of the jungle. The ground was covered with a thick carpet of dead leaves and seedling trees, though no grass or flowers were to be seen. A dense undergrowth of young trees and palms of all kinds climbed to a height of about twelve feet, obscuring the giant roots of the trees. Out of the tangled green undergrowth, however, the countless tree trunks rose straight upwards for 150 feet, where they formed a solid canopy of green that almost entirely shut out the sky. The tree trunks, though similar in that they were all of a uniform thickness and straining up towards the light, were of every colour and texture: smooth and black, scaly and ochre-red, pale grey or green with moss, some as finely dappled as a moth's wing.

The trunks were often hidden by a network of creepers which in places broke out into enormous leaves. Elsewhere, the vines and creepers hung straight down from the branches to the ground, where they had taken root again, looping themselves from tree to tree like a ship's rigging. Up in the treetops, where the great trunks suddenly burst into branches, were huge hanging gardens of moss and ferns, themselves covered in tangled webs of liana and creepers. This dense canopy of constantly rotting, regenerating, intertwining foliage provided a few windows through which the sky could be glimpsed, but it served mostly to keep out the sunlight.

In this jungle, then, the average visibility for two men standing up was at most only twenty-five yards, varying slightly from place to place. Any confidence that this might have given to the guerrillas was soon lost when they had to leave the jungle and cross a large area of open paddy-fields, where they would have been easy targets for enemy snipers.

Grateful to reach the far side of the fields, they slipped through the open trees of a rubber estate, where sunlight and fresh air were allowed in. In these isolated patches, rattans and other thorns flourished, and the palms, ferns, bracken and seedling trees became so dense that the guerrillas, male and female, had to hack their way through with their *parangs* – an exhausting task.

By midday the humidity was making them all pour sweat, and when not protected by trees they were exposed to a heat that not only beat down upon their heads but also rose in suffocating waves from the parched ground.

They soon plunged back into the jungle where, though they were protected from direct sunlight, the humidity was even more suffocating. In fact, this jungle was even worse than the one they had left. Known as *belukar*, it was land that had once been cleared but gone back to secondary jungle, with swampy thickets of thorn, bracken and bamboo even more dense and impenetrable than the original growth. Also, it contained vast stretches of swampy jungle covered with *mengkuang*, a gargantuan leathery grass with sharp blades, about twenty feet long and four or five inches wide, with a row of curved thorns along each edge. In one hour of back-breaking work, only a hundred yards would be covered.

Nevertheless, though exhausted, sweating, sometimes bleeding, and constantly attacked by vicious red ants, the patrol thought of only one thing: the successful completion of their task.

Soon they came to the outer edge of the paddy-fields, where the *kongsi*-house, or company house, of the *towkay*, the merchant who owned the estate, was located, raised high on stilts. At a nod from the leader, two of the guerrillas entered the *kongsi*-house and dragged the terrified, struggling Chinese man out. They threw him on the ground, kicked him a few times, jerked him to his knees, then bound his hands together behind his back. In this position he was given a short speech about the glories of Communism, informed that he was being punished for his anti-Communist greed, then despatched with a bullet through the head.

This first job completed, the guerrillas took a short break, during which they relaxed in the grass, eating bananas and pineapple, watching the bee-eaters and bulbuls searching for flies overhead. When the break was over, the guerrillas, who had scarcely cast a nod in the direction of the dead man, marched around the edge of the bright-green paddy-field to the kampong itself, which consisted of a few thatched houses on stilts in a grove of coconut palms, fruit trees and hibiscus flowers.

There, they forced the head of the village to provide them with a proper cooked meal – a chicken curry with *brinjol* (aubergine), eggs, fried salt fish, rice and several vegetables – followed by coffee and sweetmeats. Afterwards they tied the headman's hands behind his back, made him kneel on the ground, roped his bound hands to his tethered ankles, then made the rest of the villagers gather around him.

A couple of male guerrillas entered the headman's house and emerged carrying a table between them. Two of the females then went in and dragged out his struggling, sobbing wife.

'This man,' the leader of the guerrillas said, pointing to the trembling headman, 'is an informer who must be punished for his crimes. You will all remain here and bear witness to his punishment. Anyone who tries to leave, or turns his head away, will be shot.'

While the terrified villagers and the shocked headman looked on, the latter's wife, eight months pregnant, was thrown on to her back on the table and held down by four guerrillas. The leader of the guerrillas then withdraw his *parang*, stood at the end of the table, between the woman's outstretched feet, and raised the gleaming blade above his head.

Knowing what was about to happen, the woman writhed frantically, sobbed, vomited and gibbered like a crazed animal. She was practically insane with fear even before she felt the first, appalling cut of the blade, making her release a scream that did not sound remotely human but chilled the blood of all those who heard it.

When the patrol's leader had finished his dreadful business, leaving a horrendous mess of shredded flesh and blood on the table, he and his men melted back into the jungle.

The guerrilla leader's name was Ah Hoi, but everyone knew him as 'Baby Killer'.

1

The man emerged from the trees and stood at the far side of the road, ghostly in the cold morning mist. It was just after first light. Having been on duty all night, the young guard, British Army Private John Peterson, was dog-tired and thought he was seeing things, but soon realized that the man was real enough. He was wearing jungle-green drill fatigues, standard-issue canvas-and-rubber jungle boots and a soft jungle hat. He had a machete on one hip, an Owen sub-machine-gun slung over one shoulder and a canvas bergen, or rucksack, on his back. Even from this distance, Private Peterson could see the yellow-and-green flash of the Malayan Command badge on the upper sleeve of the man's drill fatigues.

'Jesus!' Peterson whispered softly, then turned to the other soldier in the guardhouse located to one side of the camp's main gate. 'Do you see what I see?'

The second soldier, Corporal Derek Walters, glanced through the viewing hole of the guardhouse.

'What . . .? Who the hell's *that*?'

After glancing left and right to check that nothing was coming, the ghostly soldier crossed the road. As he approached the guardhouse, it became clear that he was shockingly wasted, his fatigues practically hanging off his body, which was no more than skin and bone. Though he was heavily bearded and had blue shadows under his bloodshot eyes, both guards recognized him.

'Well, I'll be damned!' Private Peterson said. 'He actually made it!'

'Looks like it,' Corporal Peterson murmured. He opened the door of the guardhouse and stepped outside where the skeletal figure had just reached the barrier and was waiting patiently in the morning's brightening sunlight. 'Captain . . . Callaghan?' the guard asked tentatively.

'Yes, Trooper,' the captain said. 'How are you this morning?'

'Fine, boss.' Corporal Peterson shook his head in disbelief. 'Blimey, boss! You've been gone . . .'

'Three months. Raise the barrier, thanks.' When Corporal Peterson raised the barrier, Captain Patrick Callaghan grinned at him, patted him on the shoulder, then entered the sprawling combined

Army and Air Force base of Minden Barracks, Penang, where the recently reformed 22 SAS was temporarily housed.

Not that you'd know it, Callaghan thought as he walked lazily, wearily, towards headquarters where, he knew, Major Pryce-Jones would already be at his desk. While in Malaya, the SAS concealed their identity by discarding their badged beige berets and instead going out on duty in the blue berets and cap badges of the Manchester Regiment. Now, as Callaghan strolled along the criss-crossing tarmacked roads, past bunker-like concrete barracks, administration buildings raised off the ground on stilts, and flat, grassy fields, with the hangars and planes on the airstrip visible in the distance, at the base of the rolling green hills, Captain Callaghan saw men wearing every kind of beret and badge except those of the SAS.

In fact, the camp contained an exotic mix of regiments and police forces: six battalions of the Gurkha Rifles, one battalion each of the King's Own Yorkshire Light Infantry, the Seaforth Highlanders and the Devon Regiment, two battalions of the Malay Regiment, and the 26th Field Regiment of the Royal Artillery.

And that's only this camp, Callaghan thought. Indeed, just before he had left for his lone, three-month jungle patrol, a battalion of the Royal

Inniskilling Fusiliers had arrived from Hong Kong and the 2nd Guards Brigade had been sent from the United Kingdom. Subsequently, elements of other British regiments, as well as colonial troops in the form of contingents from the King's African Rifles and the Fijian Regiment, had joined in the struggle. There were now nearly 40,000 troops committed to the war in Malaya – 25,000 from Britain, including Royal Navy and Royal Air Force personnel, 10,500 Gurkhas and five battalions of the Malay Regiment.

In addition, there were the regular and armed auxiliary policemen, now totalling about 100,000 men. Most of these were Malays who had joined the Special Constabulary or served as Kampong Guards and Home Guards. The additional trained personnel for the regular police consisted mainly of men who had worked at Scotland Yard, as well as former members of the Palestine police, experienced in terrorism, men from the Hong Kong police, and even the pre-war Shanghai International Settlement, who spoke Chinese.

It's not a little war any more, Callaghan thought as he approached the headquarters building, *and it's getting bigger every day. This is a good time to be here.*

Not used to the bright sunlight, having been in the jungle so long, he rubbed his stinging eyes, forced himself to keep them open, and climbed the steps to the front of the administration block. There were wire-mesh screens across the doors and windows, with the night's grisly collection of trapped, now dead insects stuck between the wires, including mosquitoes, gnats, flies, flying beetles and spiders. An F-28 jet fighter roared overhead as Captain Callaghan, ignoring the insects' graveyard, pushed the doors open and entered the office.

With the heat already rising outside, it was a pleasure to step indoors where rotating fans created a cooling breeze over the administrative personnel – male and female; British, Malay, and some Eurasian Tamils – who were already seated at desks piled high with paper. They glanced up automatically when Callaghan entered, their eyes widening in disbelief when they saw the state of him.

'Is Major Pryce-Jones's office still here?' Callaghan asked.

'Yes, sir,' a Gurkha corporal replied. 'To your left. Down the corridor.'

'Thanks,' Callaghan replied, turning left and walking along the corridor until he came to the squadron commander's office. When he stopped in the doorway, the major raised his eyes from his desk, looked Callaghan up and down, then said in his sardonic, upper-class manner: 'It's about time you came back. You look a bloody mess, Paddy.'

'Sorry about that,' Callaghan replied, grinning broadly. He lowered his bergen and sub-machine-gun to the floor, then pulled up a chair in front of Pryce-Jones's desk. 'You know how it is.'

'If I don't, I'm sure you'll tell me in good time. Would you like a mug of hot tea?'

'That sounds wonderful, boss.'

'MARY!' Pryce-Jones's drawl had suddenly become an ear-shattering bellow directed at the pretty WRAC corporal seated behind a desk in the adjoining, smaller room.

'Yes, boss!' she replied, undisturbed.

'A tramp masquerading as an SAS officer has just entered the building, looking unwashed, exhausted and very thirsty. Tea with sugar and milk, thanks. Two of.'

'Yes, boss,' Mary said, pushing her chair back and disappearing behind the wall separating the offices.

'A sight for sore eyes,' Callaghan said.

'Bloodshot eyes,' Major Pryce-Jones corrected him. 'Christ, you look awful! Your wife would kill me for this.'

Callaghan grinned, thinking of Jennifer back in their home near Hereford and realizing that he hadn't actually thought about her for a very long

16

time. 'Oh, I don't know, boss. She thinks I'm just a Boy Scout at heart. She got used to it long ago.'

'Not to seeing you in this state,' Pryce-Jones replied. 'Pretty rough, was it?'

Callaghan shrugged. 'Three months is a long time to travel alone through the jungle. On the other hand, I saw a lot during my travels, so the time wasn't wasted.'

'I should hope not,' Pryce-Jones said.

After spending three months virtually alone in the jungle, living like an animal and trying to avoid the murderous guerrillas, most men would have expected slightly more consideration from their superior officers than Callaghan was getting. But he wasn't bothered, for this was the SAS way and he certainly had only admiration for his feisty Squadron Commander. For all his urbane ways, Pryce-Jones was a hard-drinking, hard-fighting idealist, a tough character who had won a double blue at Cambridge and given up a commission early in World War Two in order to join a Scots Guards ski battalion destined for Finland. His wartime service included three years in Burma, much of it behind Japanese lines. He had then commanded an SAS squadron in north-west Europe from late 1944 until the regiment was disbanded in 1945.

Pryce-Jones was a stranger to neither the jungle nor danger. In fact, in 1950, General Sir John

Harding, Commander-in-Chief of Far East Land Forces, had called him for a briefing on the explosion of terrorism in Malaya, asking him to produce a detailed analysis of the problem. In order to do this, Pryce-Jones had gone into the jungle for six months, where he had hiked some 1,500 miles, unescorted, in guerrilla-infested territory, and talked to most of those conducting the campaign. Though ambushed twice, he had come out alive.

According to what he had later told Callaghan, much of his time had been spent with the infantry patrols trawling through the jungle in pursuit of an 'invisible' enemy. Because of this, he had concluded that the only way to win the war was to win the hearts and minds of the population, rather than try to engage an enemy that was rarely seen. The Communist Terrorists, or CT, were following Mao Tse-tung's philosophy of moving through the peasant population like 'fish in a sea', then using them as a source of food, shelter and potential recruits. What the British had to do, therefore, was 'dry up the sea'.

To this end, Pryce-Jones's recommendation was that as many of the aboriginals as possible be relocated to villages, forts, or kampongs protected by British and Federation of Malaya forces. By so doing they would win the hearts and minds of the people, who would appreciate being protected, while simultaneously drying up the 'sea' by depriving the guerrillas of food and new recruits.

When his recommendations had met with approval, Pryce-Jones, as the OC (officer commanding) of A Squadron in Minden Barracks, had sent Callaghan into the jungle to spend three months supervising the relocation of the kampongs and checking that the defence systems provided for them and the hearts-and-minds campaign were working out as planned.

Throughout that three months Callaghan had, like Pryce-Jones before him, travelled alone, from one kampong to the other, avoiding guerrilla patrols and mostly living off the jungle, covered in sweat, drenched by rain, often waist-deep in the swamps, drained of blood by leeches, bitten by every imaginable kind of insect, often going hungry for days, and rarely getting a decent night's sleep.

In fact, it had been a nightmare, but since Pryce-Jones had done the same thing for twice that long, Callaghan wasn't about to complain.

'It wasn't that difficult,' he lied as the pretty WRAC corporal, Mary Henderson, brought in their cups of tea, passed them out and departed with an attractive swaying of her broad hips. 'Although there are slightly over four hundred villages, most are little more than shanty towns, inhabited by Chinese squatters. Before we could move them, however, we had to build up a rapport with the aboriginals – in other words, to use *your* words, win their hearts and minds. This we did by seducing them with free food, medical treatment, and protection from the CT. Medical treatment consisted mainly of primitive clinics and dispensing penicillin to cure the aborigines of yaws, a skin disease. The kampongs and troops were resupplied by river patrols in inflatable craft supplied by US special forces, or by fixed-wing aircraft, though we hope to be using helicopters in the near future.'

'Excellent. I believe you also made contact with the CT.'

'More than once, yes.'

'And survived.'

'Obviously.'

Pryce-Jones grinned. 'Men coming back from there brought us some strange stories.'

'Oh?'

'Yes. Your clandestine warfare methods raised more than a few eyebrows back here – not to mention in Britain.'

'You mean the prostitutes?'

'Exactly.'

'The best is the enemy of the good. We did what we had to do, and we did our best.'

Pryce-Jones was referring to the fact that some

of the kampong prostitutes had been asking their clients for payment in guns, grenades and bullets instead of cash, then passing them on to the guerrillas in the jungle. Learning of this, Callaghan had used some of his SF (Security Forces) troops, there to protect the kampongs, to pose as clients in order to 'pay' the prostitutes with self-destroying weapons, such as hand-grenades fitted with instantaneous fuses that would kill their users, and bullets that exploded in the faces of those trying to fire them.

'What other dirty tricks did you get up to?' Pryce-Jones asked.

'Booby-trapped food stores.'

'Naturally – but what about the mail? I received some garbled story about that.'

Now it was Callaghan's turn to grin. 'I got the idea of mailing incriminating notes or money to leading Communist organizers. The poor bastards were then executed by their own kind on the suspicion that they'd betrayed their comrades.'

'How perfectly vile.'

'Though effective.'

'Word about those dirty tricks got back to Britain and caused a great deal of outrage.'

'Only with politicians. They express their outrage in public, but in private they just want us to win, no matter how we do it. They always want it both ways.'

Pryce-Jones sighed. 'Yes, I suppose so.' He sipped his steaming tea and licked his upper lip. 'But *are* we winning?' he asked.

'Yes,' Callaghan replied without hesitation. 'The war in the jungle's definitely turned in our favour. The CT groups have become more fragmented. An awful lot of their leaders have been captured or killed. Food's scarce outside the protected kampongs and the CT are therefore finding it more difficult to find recruits among the aboriginals, most of whom are now siding with us and clinging to the protection of our secured villages and forts. Unfortunately, now that the CT propaganda has failed, they're turning to terror and committing an increasing number of atrocities.'

'You're talking about Ah Hoi.'

'Yes. Only recently that bastard disembowelled an informer's pregnant wife in front of the whole damned village. He left the villagers terrified. Now he's rumoured to be somewhere south-west of Ipoh and we'll soon have to pursue him. What shape are the men in?'

'Better than the first bunch,' Pryce-Jones replied.

Callaghan knew just what he meant. After Pryce-Jones had submitted his recommendations regarding the war, Lieutenant-Colonel 'Mad Mike'

Calvert, veteran of the Chindit campaigns in Burma and commander of the World War Two SAS (Special Air Service) Brigade, had been asked to create a special military force that could live permanently in the jungle, to deny the guerrillas sanctuary or rest. That special force, based on the original World War Two SAS, was known as the Malayan Scouts.

Some of those who volunteered for the new unit were useful veterans of the SOE (Special Operations Executive), the SAS and the Ferret Force, the latter being a paramilitary unit drawn from Army volunteers, and former members of SOE's Force 136. The 'Ferret' scouts had led fighting patrols from regular infantry battalions, making the first offensive sweeps into the jungle, aided by forty-seven Dyak trackers, the first of many such Iban tribesmen from Borneo. Though doing enough to prove that the British did not have to take a purely defensive position, the Force was disbanded when many of its best men had to return to their civilian or more conventional military posts.

Unfortunately, too many of the men recruited in a hurry were either simply bored or were persistent troublemakers whose units were happy to see them go elsewhere. One group had even consisted of ten deserters from the French Foreign Legion who had escaped by swimming ashore from a troop-ship conveying them to the war in Indo-China. To make matters worse, due to the speed with which the Malayan Emergency built up, there was little time to properly select or train them.

Shortly after the arrival of that first batch, there were official complaints about too much drunkenness and the reckless use of firearms on the base. According to Pryce-Jones, such charges had been exaggerated because of the nature of the training, which was done under dangerously realistic conditions. Nevertheless, if not as bad as described, the first recruits were certainly rowdy and undisciplined.

Some of the wilder men had eventually been knocked into shape, but others had proved to be totally unsuitable for the special forces and were gradually weeded out. Seeking a better class of soldier, 'Mad Mike' Calvert had travelled 22,000 miles in twenty-one days, including a trip to Rhodesia which led to the creation of C Squadron from volunteers in that country. From Hong Kong he brought Chinese interpreters and counter-guerrillas, who had served with him in Burma, to join his Intelligence staff. Another source was a squadron of SAS Reservists and Territorials (many of whom had served under David Stirling), which had formed up in 1947 as 21 SAS Regiment. Most of those men had been of much better calibre and proved a worthy catch when, in 1952, the

Malayan Scouts were renamed as the 22nd Special Air Service Regiment (22 SAS).

The original three squadrons, A, B, and C, that had formed 22 SAS, had been augmented by a fourth, D Squadron, before Calvert left for the UK. By 1956 a further squadron, the Parachute Regiment Squadron, was raised from volunteers drawn from the Paras. That same year, C Squadron returned to Rhodesia to become the Rhodesian SAS and was replaced by a New Zealand squadron. This Kiwi connection meant that a number of Fijians joined the Regiment.

'Do you still have problems controlling them?' Callaghan asked. 'If you do, they'll be no good in the jungle. The CT will just eat them up.'

'There's still a lot of hard drinking and the occasional fragging of officers,' Pryce-Jones replied, 'but the lack of discipline has been corrected and replaced with excellent soldiering. Unfortunately, it'll be a long time yet before we live down the reputation we acquired during those early years. Not that it bothers me. We're supposed to be different from the greens, so let's keep it that way.'

'Hear, hear,' Callaghan said, mockingly clapping his hands together. 'The question is, can we actually *use* them or are they still being used for policing duties?'

'Things have greatly improved on that front,'

Pryce-Jones told him. 'Due to the recent expansion of the Federation of Malaya Police and the creation of Home Guard units and a Special Constabulary, the Army is increasingly being released from its policing obligations and given more time and means to fight the CT. The men are all yours now.'

'They'll need to be separated from the greens,' Callaghan said, referring to the green-uniformed regular Army, 'and preferably trained in isolation.'

'I've anticipated that. A new Intelligence section has been opened in Johore. It's filled with men experienced in jungle operations from the time they worked with me in Burma. I've included Hong Kong Chinese to act as interpreters. The head of the section is Major John M. Woodhouse, Dorset Regiment. As so much of the SAS work involves a hearts-and-minds campaign, which requires Intelligence gathering of all kinds, and since we'll need Chinese speakers, the Regiment will be flown to Johore, where a special training camp is already in the process of completion. The men can complete their preliminary training here, then move on to Johore a week from now.'

'Excellent,' Callaghan said. Restless already, even though exhausted, he stood up and went to the window behind the major's desk. Looking out, he saw a Sikh foreman supervising some Malay coolies in the building of a sangar at the edge of the runway containing rows of Beverley transports and F-28 jets. The sun was rising quickly in the sky, flooding the distant landscape of green hills and forest with brilliant light.

'I want to get that bastard Ah Hoi,' he said.

'You will in due course,' Pryce-Jones replied. 'Right now, you need a good meal, a hot shower and a decent sleep. And I need to work. So get out of here, Paddy.'

'Yes, boss,' Captain Callaghan said. He picked up his soaked, heavy bergen and camouflaged sub-machine-gun, then, with a blinking of weary eyes, walked out of the office.

'You can smell him from here,' Mary said, when Callaghan had left.

'A rich aroma,' Pryce-Jones replied.

2

As Captain 'Paddy' Callaghan was having a good sleep after showering three months of jungle filth off his emaciated body, the latest influx of recently badged troopers to 22 SAS were settling in for a week of initial training in Minden Barracks, before being flown on to Johore. Though just off the Hercules C-130 transport aircraft which had flown them all the way from Bradbury Lines, Merebrook Camp, Worcestershire, via RAF Lyneham, Wiltshire, the men were in a good mood as they adjusted to the brilliant morning sunshine and rising heat of the mainland, just across the Malacca Straits, facing the lively town of Penang.

'I've heard all about that place from an RAF buddy stationed at Butterworth,' Trooper Dennis 'the Menace' Dudbridge said, as the Bedford truck transported them away from the airstrip to the barracks at the far side of a broad, flat field. Formerly of the Gloucestershire Regiment, he was short, broad-shouldered, and as feisty as a bantam cock, with a permanently split lip and broken nose from one too many pub fights. 'He said the whores all look as sexy as Marilyn Monroe.'

'If a different colour and a bit on the slit-eyed side,' Corporal 'Boney Maronie' Malone reminded him.

'I get a hard-on just *thinking* about Marilyn Monroe,' Trooper Pete Welsh informed them in his deadly serious manner.

'Put splints on it, do you?' Boney Maronie asked him.

'We can't all walk around all day with three legs,' Pete replied, brushing his blond hair from his opaque, slightly deranged blue eyes. 'Not like you, Boney.'

'He doesn't need splints,' Trooper Alf Laughton observed. 'He needs a sling to keep it off the fucking ground when it sticks out too far. Isn't that true, Boney?'

'Some of us just happen to be well endowed. Not that I'm one to boast, lads, but you just don't compare.'

'I trust you'll put it to good use in Penang,' Dennis the Menace said.

'If we get there,' Boney replied. 'I've heard they're not giving us any time off before they send us into that fucking jungle to get bled dry by leeches.'

'They wouldn't dare!' Alf Laughton exclaimed. With flaming red hair and a face pitted by acne, Laughton looked like a wild man. He had been here three years ago, with the King's Own Yorkshire Light Infantry, and still had fond memories of George Town when the sun had gone down. 'We're entitled to a little fun and games before they work us to death.'

'We're entitled to Sweet FA,' Pete Welsh said, 'and that's what we'll get.'

Though they had all been badged recently, most of these men were experienced and had come to the SAS from units active in other theatres of operation. Some had come from the Long Range Desert Group (LRDG) and the wartime SAS, others had been recruited by 'Mad Mike' Calvert from British forces stationed in the Far East; and many, including a number of National Servicemen, were skilled soldiers who had volunteered to avoid the discipline of the more conventional regular Army. At least one of them, Sergeant Ralph Lorrimer, now sitting up front beside the driver of the Bedford, had experience in guerrilla warfare gleaned from wartime operations in North Africa, and as a member of Force 136, the clandestine resistance force set up by the SOE in Malaya during the Japanese occupation. Most of them, then, were experienced men.

Indeed, one of the few with no previous experience in warfare was the recently badged Trooper Richard Parker, already nicknamed 'Dead-eye Dick' because of his outstanding marksmanship, as displayed not only during his three years with the 2nd Battalion, Royal Regiment of Fusiliers, but also on the firing range of the SAS base at Merebrook Camp, Malvern. Brown-haired, grey-eyed and almost virginally handsome, Dead-eye was as quiet as a mouse, every bit as watchful, and very keen to prove himself with the SAS. Perhaps it was because his quiet nature seemed at odds with his remarkable skills as a soldier, which included relentless tenacity as well as exceptional marksmanship, that the men had taken him up as a sort of squadron mascot and were inclined to be protective of him, particularly when out on the town. Even the traditional bullshit, when it flew thick and fast, landed lightly on young Trooper Parker.

'Hey, Dead-eye,' Boney Maronie said to him, 'when they give us some time off I'll take you into George Town and find you a nice Malayan girl who likes breaking in cherry-boys.'

'I'm not a cherry-boy,' Parker replied quietly as the Bedford bounced over a hole on the road leading to the barracks. 'I've had my fair share.'

'Oh, really?' Boney asked with a broad grin. He was six foot tall, pure muscle and bone, and sex-mad. 'Where and when was that, then?'

Dead-eye shrugged. 'Here and there. Back home. In West Croydon.'

'In your car?'

'I've never had a car.'

'So where did you do it?'

'None of your business, Boney. Where I did it and who I did it with is my concern, thanks.'

'You're a cherry-boy. Admit it!'

'I'm not,' Dead-eye replied. 'It's just something I don't talk about. I was brought up that way.'

'You bleedin' little liar,' Boney said. 'If you've got as far as squeezing a bit of tit, I'd be bloody amazed.'

Dead-eye shrugged, but said no more. The conversation was beneath him. In fact, he was attractive, girls liked him a lot, and he'd practised sex with the same clinical detachment he brought to everything else, getting his fair share. He just didn't think it worth boasting about. Being a soldier, particularly in the SAS, was much more important.

'It's the quiet little buggers like Dead-eye,' Dennis the Menace said to Boney Maronie, 'who get their oats while blow-hards like you are farting into the wind. I know who *I'd* bet on.'

'Hey, come on . . .' Boney began, but was rudely interrupted when the Bedford ground to a halt outside the barracks and Sergeant Lorrimer bawled: 'All out back there! Shift your lazy arses!'

The men did as they were ordered, hopping off the back and sides of the open Bedford MK four-ton truck. When they were assembled on the baking-hot tarmac in front of the barracks, Sergeant Lorrimer pointed to the unattractive concrete blocks and said: 'Argue among yourselves as to who gets what basha, then put your kit in the lockers and have a brief rest. I'll be back in about thirty minutes to give you further instructions.'

'The man said *a brief rest*,' Pete Welsh echoed, 'and he obviously means it.'

'You have a complaint, Trooper?' Sergeant Lorrimer placed his large hands on his hips and narrowed his eyes. He was sweating and his beefy face was flushed.

'Complain? I wouldn't dream of it, boss! Thirty minutes is much too long.'

'Then we'll make it twenty,' Lorrimer said. 'I take it you agree that's in order?'

'Absolutely!' Welsh glanced uneasily left and right as the rest of the men groaned audibly and glared at him. 'No problem here, boss.'

'I could do with some scran,' Dennis the Menace said.

33

'You'll get a proper meal tonight,' Sergeant Lorrimer replied, 'when you've been kitted out and had a sermon from the OC. Meanwhile, you'll have to content yourself with a breakfast of wads and a brew up. And since you've only got twenty minutes to eat and drink, I suggest you get started.'

Sergeant Lorrimer jumped back up into the Bedford while the men moaned and groaned. Even as the truck was heading away towards the administration buildings located along the edge of the airstrip, the men continued complaining.

'Your bloody fault, Pete,' Dennis the Menace said. 'We could have had all of thirty minutes – now we're cut down to twenty. You should've known better.'

'I only said . . .'

'One word too many.' Alf Laughton was disgusted with him. 'You know what Sergeant Lorrimer's like when he gets too much sunshine. His face turns purple and he can't stand the bullshit.'

'You're all wasting time talking,' Dead-eye pointed out with his usual grasp of the priorities. 'If you keep talking you'll waste more of your twenty minutes and won't have time for breakfast. Let's pick beds and unpack.'

The accommodation consisted of rectangular concrete bunkers surrounded by flat green fields, slightly shaded by papaya and palm trees. The buildings had wire-mesh and wooden shutters instead of glass windows. The shutters were only closed during tropical storms; the wire-mesh was there to keep out the many flying insects attracted by the electric lights in the evenings. Likewise, because of the heat, the wooden doors were only closed during storms.

From any window of the barracks the men could see the airstrip, with F-28 jets, Valetta, Beverley and Hercules C-130 transports, as well as Sikorski S-55 Whirlwind helicopters, taking off and landing near the immense, sun-scorched hangars. Beyond the airstrip was a long line of trees, marking the edge of the jungle.

After selecting their beds and transferring personal kit to the steel lockers beside each bed, the men hurriedly unwrapped their prepacked wads, or sandwiches, and had hot tea from vacuum flasks.

'Christ, it's hot,' Pete Welsh said, not meaning the tea.

'It's hardly started,' Alf Laughton told him. 'Early hours yet. By noon you'll be like a boiled lobster, no matter how you try to avoid the sun. Fucking scorching, this place is.'

'I want to see Penang,' Dennis the Menace said. 'All those things you told us about it, Alf. All them Malay and Chinese birds in their *cheongsams*, slit up to the hip. George Town, here I come!'

'When?' Boney Maronie asked. 'If we're not even getting lunch on our first day here, what hope for George Town? We're gonna be worked to death, mates.'

'I don't mind,' Dead-eye said, stowing the last of his personal gear in his steel locker. 'I came here to fight a war – not to get pissed and screw some whores. I want to see some action.'

Dennis the Menace grinned crookedly and placed his hand affectionately on Dead-eye's head. 'What a nice lad you are,' he said, only mocking a little. 'And what a good trooper! It's good to see you're so keen.'

'You'd see action if you came with me to George Town,' Boney Maronie informed him. 'You'd see a battle or two, mate.'

'Not the kind of battle Dead-eye wants to see,' Dennis the Menace said. 'This kid here has higher aims.'

'That's right,' Dead-eye said.

Boney Maronie was rolling his eyes in mock disgust when the red-faced Sergeant Lorrimer returned, this time in an updated 4×4 Willys jeep that had armoured perspex screens and a Browning 0.5-inch heavy machine-gun mounted on the front. Hopping down, leaving the driver behind the

steering wheel, Lorrimer bawled instructions for
the men to assemble outside the barracks in order
of height. When they had done so, he marched
them across the broad green field bordered with
papaya and palm trees to the quartermaster's store,
to be kitted out with everything they needed except
weapons, which could only be signed for when
specifically required.

The standard-issue clothing included jungle-
green drill fatigues, a matching soft hat and
canvas-and-rubber boots. The men were also supplied with special canvas bergens which looked
small when rolled up, but enormous when filled.
The contents of each individual bergen included
a sleeping bag of hollow-fill, man-made fibre; a
bivi-bag, or waterproof one-man sheet used as a
temporary shelter; a portable hexamine stove and
blocks of hexamine fuel; an aluminium mess tin,
mug and utensils; a brew kit, including sachets of
tea, powdered milk and sugar; matches in a waterproof container and flint for when the matches ran
out; needles and thread; a fishing line and hooks;
a pencil torch and batteries; a luminous button
compass; signal flares; spare radio batteries;
fluorescent marker panels for spotter planes in case
of rescue; a magnifying glass to help find splinters
and stings in the skin; and a medical kit containing sticking plasters, bandages, cotton wool,

antiseptic, intestinal sedative, antibiotics, antihistamine, water-sterilizing tablets, anti-malaria tablets,
potassium permanganate, analgesic, two surgical
blades and butterfly sutures.

'Just let me at you,' Dennis the Menace said,
waving one of his small surgical blades in front
of Boney's crutch. 'The world'll be a lot safer if
you don't have one, so let's lop it off.'

'Shit, Dennis!' Boney yelled, jumping back and
covering his manhood with his hands. 'Don't piss
around like that!'

'You think this is funny, Trooper?' Sergeant
Lorrimer said to Dennis the Menace. 'You think
we give you these items for your amusement,
do you?'

'Well, no, boss, I was just . . .'

'Making a bloody fool of yourself, right?'
Lorrimer shoved his beetroot-red face almost
nose to nose with the trooper. 'Well, let me tell
you, that where you're going you might find a lot
of these items useful – particularly when you have
to slice a poisonous spike or insect out of your
own skin, or maybe slash open a snake bite, then
suck the wound dry and suture it yourself without
anaesthetic. Will you be laughing then, Trooper?'

'No, boss, I suppose not. I mean, I . . .'

'Damn right, you won't, Trooper. A joker like
you – you'll probably be pissing and shitting

yourself, and crying for your mummy's tit. So don't laugh at this kit!'

'Sorry, boss,' Dennis the Menace said. 'Hear you loud and clear, boss.'

'At least I know you clean the wax from your ears,' Lorrimer said, then bellowed: 'Move it, you men!'

Once the squadron had been clothed and kitted out in order of size, they were marched back across the broad field, which, at the height of noon, had become a veritable furnace that burned their skin and made them pour sweat. To this irritation was added the midges and mosquitoes, the flies and flying beetles, none of which could be swotted away because every man, apart from being burdened with his heavy bergen, also had his hands engaged carrying even more equipment. When eventually they reached the barracks, their instinct was to throw the kit on the floor and collapse on their bashas. But this was not to be.

'Right!' Sergeant Lorrimer bawled. 'Stash that kit, have a five-minute shower, put on your drill fatigues, and reassemble outside fifteen minutes from now. OK, you men, *shake out!*'

The latter command was SAS slang for 'Prepare for combat', but the men knew exactly what Lorrimer meant by using it now: they were going to get no rest. Realizing that this time they didn't even have time to complain or bullshit, they fought each other for the few showers, hurriedly dressed, and in many cases were assembling outside without having dried themselves properly, their wet drill fatigues steaming dry in the burning heat. They were still steaming when Lorrimer returned in the jeep, but this time he waved the jeep away, then made the men line up in marching order.

'Had your scran, did you?' he asked when they were lined up in front of him.

'Yes, boss!' the men bawled in unison.

'Good. 'Cause that's all you're going to get until this evening. You're here to work – not wank or chase skirt – and any rest you thought you might be having, you've already had in that Hercules. OK, follow me.'

He marched them across the flat field, through eddying heatwaves, all the way back to the armoury, located near the quartermaster's stores. There they were given a selection of small arms, including the M1 0.3in carbine with 30-round detachable magazines, which was good for low-intensity work at short range, but not much else; the 9mm Owen sub-machine-gun, which used 33-round, top-mounted box magazines, could fire at a rate of 700 rounds per minute, and was reliable and rugged; the relatively new 7.62mm semi-automatic SLR (self-loading rifle) with 20-round light box magazines, which had yet to prove its worth; and the standard-issue Browning 9mm High Power handgun with 13-round magazines and Len Dixon holster.

When the weapons had been distributed among the men, each given as much as he could carry, Lorrimer pointed to the Bedford truck parked near by.

'Get in that,' he said. 'After the weather in England, I'm sure you'll appreciate some sunshine. All right, *move it*!'

When they had all piled into the Bedford, they were driven straight to the firing range, where they spent the whole afternoon, in ever-increasing heat, firing the various weapons – first the M1 carbine, then the Owen sub-machine-gun and finally the unfamiliar SLR. The heat was bad enough, but the insects were even worse, and within an hour or two most of the men were nearly frantic, torn between concentrating on the weapons and swotting away their tormentors. When they attempted to do the latter, they were bawled at by the redoubtable Sergeant Lorrimer. After two hours on the range, which seemed more like twelve, their initial enthusiasm for the sunlight, which had seemed so wonderful after England, waned dramatically, leaving them with the realization that they had been travelling a long time and now desperately needed sleep, proper food, and time to acclimatize to this new environment.

'What the fuck's the matter with you, Trooper?' Sergeant Lorrimer demanded of Pete Welsh.

'Sorry, boss, but I just can't keep my eyes open.'

'A little tired after your long journey from England, are you?' Lorrimer asked sympathetically.

'Yes, boss.'

'So what are you going to do in the jungle, Trooper, when you have to sleep when standing waist-deep in water? Going to ask for tea and sympathy, are you? Perhaps some time off?'

'I'm not asking now, boss. I'm just having problems in keeping my eyes open. It's the sunlight, combined with the lack of sleep. We're all the same, boss.'

'Oh, I see,' Lorrimer said. 'You're *all* the same. Well, that makes all the difference!' He glanced melodramatically around him, at the other men lying belly-down on the firing range, half asleep when not being tormented by mosquitoes and other dive-bombing tormentors. 'Need sleep, do you?' he asked.

'Yes, boss!' they all bawled simultaneously.

'If you sleep before bedtime,' Lorrimer explained,

42

'you'll all wake up in the middle of the morning, so you'd best stay awake. *On your feet, Troopers*!'

When they jumped to their feet, shocked by the tenor of Lorrimer's voice, he ran them a few times around the firing range, which was now like God's anvil, and only let them rest again when at least one of them, the normally tough Alf Laughton, started swaying as if he'd been poleaxed.

'Get back in the Bedford,' Lorrimer said, addressing the whole group. 'You're just a bunch of pansies.'

Breathless, pouring sweat, hardly able to focus their eyes, they piled into the Bedford, were driven back to the armoury, lined up for what seemed like hours to return their weapons, then were allowed to make their own way back to the barracks. There, in a state of near collapse, most of them threw themselves down on their steel-framed beds.

No sooner had they done so than Sergeant Lorrimer appeared out of nowhere, bawling, 'Off your backs, you lot! You think this is Butlins? Get showered and change into your dress uniforms and be at the mess by 5.30 sharp. Any man not seen having dinner will be up for a fine. Is that understood? *Move it*!'

They did so. In a state of virtual somnambulism, they turned up at the crowded mess, where Sergeant Lorrimer was waiting to greet them.

'Spick and span,' he said, looking them up and down with an eagle eye. 'All set for scran. OK, go in and get fed, take your time about it, but make sure you reassemble back out here. No pissing off to the NAAFI.'

'The day's over after din-dins,' Dennis the Menace said.

'It is for the common soldier,' Lorrimer replied, 'but not for you lot.' He practically purred with anticipation. 'You lot are *privileged*!'

They soon found out what he meant. After dinner, which few of them could eat, being far too exhausted, they were marched back to the barracks, told to change back into their already filthy drill fatigues, then driven out of the camp in a Bedford. A good ten miles from the camp, in an area notable only for the anonymity of its jungle landscape – no towns, no kampongs – they were dropped off in pairs, each a few miles from the other, none having the slightest clue where they were, and told that if they wanted a good night's sleep, they had to make their own way back to the camp as best they could. If they were not back by first light, when Reveille would be called, they would be RTU'd – sent straight back to Blighty.

'Do we get even a compass?' Boney Maronie asked. He and Pete Welsh were one of the first pairs to be dropped off.

'No,' Lorrimer replied. 'What you get is the information that the camp is approximately ten miles north, south, east or west. The rest you have to find out for yourself. Have a nice evening, Trooper.'

'Thanks, boss. Same to you.'

In fact, all of them made it back, though by very different means. Boney Maronie and Peter Welsh marched until they came to a main road – an hour's difficult hike in itself – then simply hitched a lift from a Malay banker whose journey home took him straight past the camp. Dennis the Menace and Dead-eye Dick had checked the direction of their journey in the Bedford, so they simply used the moon to give them an east-west reference and used that to guide them back the way they had come. After a walk that took them well past midnight, they came to a kampong where the headman, obviously delighted to have a chat with strangers, gave them dinner then drove them back to the base, depositing them there two hours before first light. Alf Laughton, dropped off with a recently badged trooper, formerly of the King's Own Scottish Borderers, became disgusted with his young partner, deliberately lost him, then waylaid a passing cyclist, beat him unconscious, stole his bicycle and cycled most of the way back. Just before reaching the main gate of the camp, he dumped the bicycle and walked the rest of the way, thus ensuring that neither the assault nor the theft could be traced back to him.

Others did even worse than Alf Laughton and, being found out, were RTU'd, as was Laughton's unfortunate young partner.

The rest, getting back successfully without committing any known criminal act, collapsed immediately on their beds and slept as long as they could. The ones who had the longest sleep were Boney Maronie and Pete Welsh, who had managed to get back two hours after leaving, earning almost a whole night in a proper bed.

Few others were so lucky. Typical were Dennis the Menace and Dead-eye Dick, who, having not slept since leaving England nearly twenty-six hours earlier, managed to get two hours sleep before Reveille, at first light. After that, the whole murderous routine was repeated again – for seven relentless, soul-destroying days.

All of this was merely a build-up to Johore, where, so Sergeant Lorrimer assured them, the 'real' jungle training would be done.

Johore loomed like a nightmare of the kind that only this breed of man could fully understand and hope to deal with.

3

The troopers coped with the forthcoming night-mare of Johore by fantasizing about the great time they would have when they were given the mandatory weekend off and could spend it on the island of Penang. This fantasy was fuelled by the stories of Alf Laughton, who, having been in Malaya before, when serving with the King's Own Yorkshire Light Infantry, still recalled vividly his wild evenings in George Town, with its trishaws, taxis, steaming food stalls, colourful markets and bazaars, sleazy bars, grand hotels and, of course, incredibly beautiful Eurasian women in sexy *cheongsams*.

Alf Laughton had the rest of them salivating.

The first seven days, which seemed like seven years, ended on a Friday and most of them, though exhausted beyond what they could have imagined, were looking forward to their great weekend in Penang, after their briefing by Major Pryce-Jones, which took place, helpfully, at six in the evening, when the sun was going down and the humid air was cooling.

'First, a bit of background,' Pryce-Jones began. He was standing on a raised section of the floor at one end of the room, in front of a large map of Malaya. Captain Callaghan was seated in a chair to the side of the raised area. In the week he had been back, he had already put on weight and was looking more his normal, healthy self. 'The Communist Party has existed here in a small way since the 1930s,' Pryce-Jones continued, 'when this was a prosperous place. Unfortunately, we then made the mistake of arming the Communist guerrillas during the war, to enable them to fight the Japanese. It never entered our heads that after the war those same weapons would be turned against us. In the event, they were. Once the guerrilla supremo, Chin Peng, had been awarded an OBE in the Victory Honours, he formed his 1,200 wartime guerrillas into ten regiments and used his 4,000 captured British and Japanese weapons to mount a campaign of terror against the Malays. They publicly executed rubber plantation workers, lectured the horrified onlookers on the so-called war against Imperialism, then melted back into the jungle.'

After pausing to let his words sink in, Pryce-Jones

tapped the blackboard beside the map, where someone had scrawled in white chalk: '*Kill one, frighten
a thousand:* Sun-Zu.'

'These are the words of the old Chinese warrior
Sun-Zu, and Chin Peng's guerrillas live by them.
For this reason, once they had struck terror into the
hearts of the Malays, they turned on the Europeans,
mostly British plantation managers. Two were
bound to chairs and ritually murdered. After that,
the war escalated dramatically and British forces
were brought in.'

Pryce-Jones put the pointer down and turned
away from the blackboard. 'By early 1950, the
Communist Terrorists had killed over 800 civilians,
over 300 police officers and approximately 150
soldiers. We can take comfort from the fact that
over 1,000 CT have been killed, over 600 have
been captured, and nearly 400 have surrendered
so far. Nevertheless, there's no sign of an end to
the war, which is why you men are here.'

'Lucky us!' Dennis the Menace exclaimed, copping
a couple of laughs.

'The CT attacks,' Pryce-Jones continued when
the laughter had died away, 'are mostly against
kampongs, isolated police stations, telecommuni-
cations, railways, buses, rubber estates, tin mines,
and what they term the "running dogs of the
British" – namely, us, the Security Forces. British

infantry, however, with the help of Gurkha and police patrols, have managed to cut off food supplies going to the CT in the jungle. They've also booby-trapped supplies of rice, fish and other foods found prepared for collection by the CT. With the removal of over 400 Chinese squatters' villages from the edge of the jungle to wire-fenced enclosures defended by us, the CT have been deprived of yet another source of food, supplies and manpower. For this reason, they've moved deeper into the jungle, known to them as the *ulu*, where they're attempting to grow their own maize, rice and vegetables. In order to do this, they have to make cleared spaces in the *ulu* – and those spaces can be seen from the air. Unfortunately, it takes foot patrols days, sometimes weeks, to reach them. Which is where you come in.'

'Here it comes!' Boney Maronie chimed.

'The hard sell,' Dennis the Menace added.

'All right, you men, be quiet,' Sergeant Lorrimer told them. 'We don't have all night for this.'

Looking forward to the first evening of their free weekend, which most would spend in Penang, the men could only agree with Sergeant Lorrimer, and settled down quickly.

'To win the cooperation of the local tribesmen,' Pryce-Jones continued, 'we established a number of protected kampongs. Attracted by free food and medical treatment, as well as by the idea of protection from the atrocities of the CT, the tribesmen gradually moved into the kampongs and set up their bashas next to those of our troops. Medical supplies were dropped by the RAF and treatment given by doctors and Royal Army Medical Corps NCOs attached to the SAS. Once an individual settlement was established with a full quota of tribesmen, it became permanent and was placed under the control of the police or Malayan security forces. We'd then move on to build another elsewhere until we had a whole chain of such "forts" down the centre of the country, effectively controlling the area, keeping the terrorists out.'

'The hearts-and-minds campaign,' young Dead-eye said, having already done his homework.

'Correct. The campaign was successful in winning the trust of the tribesmen. They responded by becoming our eyes and ears in the *ulu*, passing on information on the whereabouts and movements of the CT.'

'So what's our place in all this?' Boney Maronie asked.

'You'll be called upon to be part of patrols based for long periods in the jungle,' Pryce-Jones replied. 'There you'll make contact with the aboriginals, the Sakai, who're being coerced by the terrorists into providing them with food. Once contact is made, you'll attempt to win their trust by supplying them with penicillin and other medicines, by defending their kampongs from the CT and in any other way you can.'

'Bloody nursemaids again!' Dennis the Menace groaned.

'Is staying for long periods in the jungle feasible for anyone other than the aboriginals?' Dead-eye asked quietly.

'Yes,' Captain Callaghan said. 'It's a daunting task, but it *can* be done. Indeed, at a time when seven days was considered the absolute limit for white men, one of our Scout patrols spent 103 days in there. The CC' – Callaghan nodded in the direction of Major Pryce-Jones –'has spent six months alone in the *ulu* and, as you know, I've just returned from a three-month hike through it. So it can be done.'

'If the Ruperts can do it,' Alf Laughton said, using the SAS nickname for officers, 'then I reckon we can too.'

'As Trooper Dudbridge has expressed his disdain for the hearts-and-minds side of the operation,' Pryce-Jones cut in, 'I should inform you that your main task will be to assist the Malay Police Field Force at kampongs and in jungle-edge patrols. You'll also send out small patrols from your jungle base to ambush the CT on the tracks they use to get to and from their hide-outs.'

'That sounds more like it,' Pete Welsh said, grinning as his wild blue eyes flashed from left to right and back again. 'Doing what we've been trained to do.'

'You've also been trained in hearts-and-minds tactics,' Sergeant Lorrimer reminded him, 'so don't ever forget it.'

'Sorry, boss,' Welsh replied, grinning lopsidedly and rolling his eyes at his mates. 'No offence intended.'

'Good.' Lorrimer turned away from him and spoke to Major Pryce-Jones instead. 'Will we be engaged *only* in jungle-edge patrols?'

'No,' Captain Callaghan replied after receiving the nod from Pryce-Jones. 'It's true that in the past we've avoided deep-penetration raids, but because of the increasing success of our food-denial operations, the CT are now heading deeper into the *ulu*. Unfortunately for them, in order to grow their own food they have to fell trees and make clearings. As our Company Commander has rightly pointed out, such clearings can be spotted from the air, which means they're vulnerable to attack. We'll therefore attack them. We'll do so by parachuting – or tree-jumping, which you're about to learn – into a confined Dropping Zone near the area. Then we'll place a cordon around the clearing. It won't be easy and certainly it will be dangerous, but in the end we'll win.'

'We're going to parachute into the *jungle*?' Alf Laughton asked, sounding doubtful.

'Yes,' Captain Callaghan answered. 'If I can do it, anyone can do it – and believe me, I've done it.'

'Is that one of the things we'll learn in Johore?'

'Correct,' Callaghan replied.

'I can't wait,' Pete Welsh said sarcastically. 'The top of a tree right through my nuts. I'll be back in the boys' choir.'

'Assuming that Trooper Welsh doesn't lose his precious nuts on a tree,' Sergeant Lorrimer said, 'and we all make it down to the DZ in one piece, what problems can we expect to find in that terrain?'

'Most of the country is dense and mountainous jungle,' Captain Callaghan replied, 'considered habitable only by aboriginal peoples, such as the Sakai. The hill contours make for steep, slippery climbs, while the routes off the paths are dense with trees that can trip you up and break your ankles. Nevertheless, as the few paths are likely to be mined or ambushed, you'll have to avoid them and instead move over uncharted ground. The terrorists have a network of jungle informers and will be using them to keep track of your movements, which will help them either to attack or avoid you. Finding them before they find you won't be made any easier by the difficulties of navigating in the jungle. You will, however, be aided by Dyak trackers, Iban tribesmen from Sarawak, all experts in jungle tracking and survival.'

'We go out in small patrols?' Dead-eye said.

'Yes. Three- or four-man teams. In the words of the founder of the Malayan Scouts, Lieutenant-Colonel Calvert: "The fewer you are, the more frightened you are, therefore, the more cautious you are and, therefore, the more silent you are. You are more likely to see the enemy before he will be able to see you." We abide by those words.'

'What's our first, specific mission?' Boney Maronie asked.

Callaghan stepped aside to let Major Pryce-Jones take the centre of the raised platform and give them the good news.

'Aerial reconnaissance has shown that the CT are growing food in a clearing in the Belum Valley, a remote, long mountain valley located near the Thai border. That valley will be searched by Gurkha, Commando and Malaya Police patrols, all moving in on foot, which should take them five days but gives them the advantage of being more difficult to spot. You men will form the stop, or blocking, party, parachuting in a day's march from the RV.

This operation will commence once you've completed your extensive jungle training in Johore.'

'When do we leave, boss?' Dennis the Menace asked.

'Tonight.'

4

The camp in Johore was a primitive affair, shared between Gurkhas, Royal Marines, RAF, British Army REME, Kampong Guards from the Federation of Malaya Police and SAS personnel. Hastily thrown together in a clearing in the jungle, it was surrounded by coconut palms, papaya trees and deep monsoon drains, with rows of wood-and-thatch barracks, latrines, open showers, a mess hut, armoury, quartermaster's store, motor pool, administrative block, NAAFI shop, airstrip for fixed-wing aircraft and helicopters, and a centrally located 'sports ground' with an obstacle course at one end, used for everything from weapons training to Close Quarters Battle (CQB) and unarmed combat.

'They don't even give us one night in Penang,' Alf Laughton complained as they were selecting their camp-beds and settling into the barracks, 'and now they plonk us down in this dump. A diabolical liberty!'

'More dust, heat, flies and mosquitoes,' Dennis the Menace said. 'Welcome to Paradise!'

'You know why these barracks are raised off the ground, don't you?' Pete Welsh asked rhetorically, having the answer all prepared. 'Because this place is crawling with scorpions, centipedes and snakes, every one of 'em poisonous.'

'It's crawling with everything except women,' Boney Maronie said, 'which is why they should have given us at least one night out in Penang. I think I'm getting ready to explode. I'll drench the whole fucking ceiling.'

'Boasting again,' Dennis the Menace said. 'You haven't really got it in you. But that obstacle course out there looks like hell. A few runs over that fucker and you'll soon get rid of all your excess energy. By the time you've finished, you won't remember what a woman is, let alone what she feels like.'

'Tree-jumping,' Dead-eye said. 'That's what bothers me. Those trees are 150 feet high and pretty damned dense. I don't fancy climbing those with a bergen, rifle and knotted rope, let alone parachuting into them.'

'Piece of piss,' Pete Welsh said, his grin making him look slightly crazy. 'You just spread your legs and get spiked through the balls by the top of a tree. If you miss that, you crash down through the branches and get all smashed to hell. Failing that, you snag your chute on the branches and possibly hang yourself. Sounds like a joyride.'

'I can't wait,' Alf Laughton said.

Once settled in, the men were gathered together in the briefing room, given a brief lecture on the history and habits of the jungle natives, told not to call them 'Sakai', which meant 'slave', and informed that they would be receiving a two-hour lesson in the native language every day. The first such lesson began immediately and was very demanding.

When it had ended, at 10 a.m., the men were allowed a ten-minute tea break, then marched to the armoury, where they were given a selection of weapons, including those fired on the range of Minden Barracks: the M1 0.3in carbine, the 9mm Owen sub-machine-gun, the 7.62mm semi-automatic SLR and the Browning 9mm High Power handgun. They were also given a Fairburn-Sykes commando knife and a machete-like *parang*.

Having already tested the men's skills on the range at Minden Barracks, Sergeant Lorrimer knew precisely who was best at what and distributed the weapons accordingly, with the Owen sub-machine-guns going to those he was designating as scouts, or 'point men', in his patrols.

'Here,' he told the men assembled outside the armoury in the already fierce heat, 'you won't have to sign the weapons in and out. Instead, you'll keep them with you at all times, either on your person or in your lockers. If any man loses a weapon or ammunition he'll be RTU'd instantly.'

From that moment on, though the men were trained together, they were broken up into four-man teams, first devised by David Stirling in World War Two as a means of combining minimum manpower with maximum surprise. The four-man team was deemed to be the most effective because members could pair up and look after each other, both tactically and domestically, sharing duties such as brewing up, cooking meals, erecting shelters or camouflaging their position. Also, soldiers have a natural bonding instinct and divide into pairs to tackle most tasks.

Though every member of the four-man patrols had been trained in signals, demolition and medicine, and was presently learning the rudiments of the local language, each individual had to specialize in one of these. Trained to Regimental Signaller standard in morse code and ciphers, the team's specialist signaller was responsible for calling in aerial resup (resupply) missions, casevac (casualty evacuation) and keeping contact with base. While all of the team had been trained in demolition, the team's specialist in this skill was responsible for either supervising, or carrying out, major sabotage operations. The job of the language specialist was to converse with the locals, on the one hand gaining their trust as part of the hearts-and-minds campaign, on the other gleaning from them whatever information he could. The specialist in medicine would not only look after the other members of his patrol, but also attempt to win the trust of the locals by treating them for stomach pains, toothache, tuberculosis, malaria, scurvy or any other illnesses, real or imagined.

'Though the basic unit will be the four-man team,' Captain Callaghan told them when they were kneeling in the dirt at the edge of the sports ground, in the murderous heat, assailed constantly by flying insects, 'we have three different kinds of patrol here. First is the reconnaissance patrol, usually a four-man team, which is tasked with observation and intelligence gathering, including topographical info; the selecting of sites for RVs, helicopter landings and good ambush positions; location of the enemy; and the checking of friendly defences, such as minefields. Second is the standing patrol, which can be anything from a four-man team to a troop or more. The standing patrol provides a warning of enemy advance and details of its composition, prevents enemy infiltration and directs artillery fire or ground-attack aircraft on to enemy positions. Finally, we have the fighting patrols, composed of either two four-man teams or an entire troop, depending on the nature of the mission. The job of the fighting patrol is to harass the enemy; conduct raids to gain intelligence or capture prisoners; carry out attacks against specific targets; and prevent the enemy from obtaining info about friendly forces in a given area. Sooner or later, each of you will take part in all three types of patrol. First, however, you'll undergo a weapons training programme more rigorous than anything you've imagined in your worst nightmares. They're all yours, Sergeant Lorrimer.'

Callaghan was not exaggerating. While the normal SAS training programme was the most demanding of any in the armed forces, even that had not prepared the men for the merciless demands that were now placed upon their physical stamina and skill. They were called upon not only to perform target practice in the scorching heat while being assailed by bloated flies, kamikaze mosquitoes and a host of other insects driven mad by the smell of human sweat, but also to carry out numerous tactical movements designed to meet the special requirements of jungle warfare.

Thus, when Sergeant Lorrimer was satisfied that each man had proven himself a crack shot, he moved on to lessons in the actions and drills to be carried out in case of contact with the enemy, the proper order of march when in the jungle, the silent signals required when changing formation, the various drills for encounters with natural and man-made obstacles, and, most important, the Head-On Contact Drill.

'The HOCD,' he explained as they were getting their breath back after an exhausting 'shoot and scoot' exercise, 'is the Standard Operating Procedure, or SOP, devised specially for four-man patrols on the move. When contact is made with the enemy, each member of the patrol will move instantly into a position that allows him to open fire without hitting a comrade. You four,' he said, jabbing his finger at Dennis the Menace, Boney Maronie, Dead-eye Dick and Alf Laughton. 'Stand up.'

'Jesus, boss,' Dennis the Menace complained as he wiped the sweat from his sunburnt face, 'we've just sat down for a so-called break.'

'The break's over, so get to your feet.' When the foursome were standing at the edge of the sports ground, near one of the deep monsoon drains, Lorrimer made them move into position to demonstrate a particular HOCD. He placed Dead-eye well away from the others, at the front as lead scout. Pushing the others closer together as carelessly as if they were shop-window dummies, he said: 'So! If the patrol is moving in file, these three men behind the lead scout will break left and right as they bring their weapons to bear on the enemy . . . *Break, damn it! Break!*'

Though already exhausted from their last exercise, Dennis the Menace, Boney Maronie and Alf Laughton had to quickly break apart while swinging their weapons up into the firing position.

'The patrol now has the option of advancing on the enemy or withdrawing,' Lorrimer continued. 'Should they choose the latter option, two of them will lay down covering fire . . . *Go on, then!*' he bawled at Dead-eye and Dennis the Menace, now forming a couple. '*Get on with it!*' When they had done as they were told, dropping into the kneeling position required for covering fire, then pretending to fire, much to the amusement of the onlookers, Lorrimer continued: 'So while these two are laying down covering fire, the other two will withdraw a distance . . . *Come on, you two, withdraw!*' he bawled at Boney Maronie and Alf Laughton. When they had done as ordered, withdrawing a few yards and taking up firing positions, he went on: 'The second two, as you can see, are now in a covering position, allowing the first pair to fall back – *Come on, fall back, you two!* – and so on. They keep repeating this movement until they're out of range of the enemy. You got that?'

'*Yes, boss!*' the men bawled in unison, some breaking into applause and laughter when the four returned sheepishly to the main group.

'You, you, you and you,' Lorrimer said, jabbing his finger at another four troopers. 'Get up and let's see you do it.'

That wiped the grins off their faces.

Every day was a relentless routine of early Reveille, hurried breakfast, the two-hour language lesson, ten-minute tea break, two hours on the firing range, an hour for lunch, two hours of battle tactics, both theoretical and physical, a ten-minute tea break, another two hours of Close Quarters Battle (CQB) and hand-to-hand combat, an hour for dinner, then an evening filled with map-reading, medical training, signals training and demolition.

Second best was not good enough. They had to be perfect at everything and were pushed relentlessly hard until they were.

Sergeant Lorrimer was a former Dorset Regiment and Force 136 NCO who was scarcely interested in drill and uniform, but hated sloppiness where battle discipline was concerned. When one soldier accidentally opened fire with a rifle, Lorrimer took the rifle off him, removed the safety-pin from a hand-grenade, then handed the soldier the grenade.

'Carry that for the rest of the day,' he said. 'By which time you should know how to handle a rifle.'

Lorrimer was also of the school which believes that discipline can be imposed in the good old-fashioned way – with fists – instead of with the rule book. More than once, instead of placing insolent troopers on a charge, he told them to 'step outside' to settle the matter with fisticuffs. So far, no one had managed to beat him and all of them, even when making fun of him, respected him for it.

For the most part the training was dangerously realistic. It included throwing grenades and diving for cover in the deep monsoon drains running through the area around the camp. This was only one of several lessons with live ammunition that disregarded the normal safety rules for field firing ranges. Since there was neither the time nor the facilities for such routines, all training had to take place on the parade ground and other clear spaces near the camp.

The working day usually ended at 10 p.m., leaving the men a couple of hours in which to do as they wished. As there was nowhere to go – outside the camp there was only jungle – they drank a lot of beer, became drunk quite quickly after the heat and exertion of the day and often got up to boyish pranks and fights.

The latter appeared to be the speciality of Pete Welsh and Alf Laughton, both of whom were hot-tempered and given to violent outbursts of the kind that would soon be outlawed by the Regiment.

'I'd trust those two fuckers about as far as I could throw them,' Dennis the Menace said. 'The NCOs in their parent regiments encouraged them to apply for the SAS just to get rid of them. A pair of troublemakers, if you ask me.'

'I'm not asking,' Boney Maronie replied. 'The less we know, the better, mate.'

Often, when there were fights, they were broken up by Sergeant Lorrimer, whose offer to try their luck with him outside would nearly always turn the men's anger into laughter and usually lead them to shake hands. Nevertheless, he complained privately to Captain Callaghan about the number of unsuitable men they had had wished upon them.

'We're gradually weeding them out,' Callaghan reassured him, 'but it's going to take a bit more time. In the meantime, we have to deal with what we've got and just pray that they don't cause too much trouble.'

'I don't believe in prayer,' Lorrimer replied, 'and I still think we're taking a big chance with some of those men.'

A week after arriving at Johore, with their preliminary training completed successfully, the men were moved out of the camp to live in primitive conditions and acquire new skills from the indigenous aboriginals and from Iban trackers brought to Malaya from Sarawak. Their first lessons were in the use of the *parang*, which was indispensable for hacking a path through dense undergrowth. Its use called for a surprisingly high degree of skill, and in the course of learning this many of the men cut themselves badly.

Wounded or not, they were then taught tracking in the jungle and swamps. This was a particularly exhausting business, requiring constant observation and concentration. While a top speed of approximately a mile an hour could be attained in a jungle environment, this was discouraged as it could mean missing vital clues about the passage and location of the enemy. Instead, a slow, cautious, ever-vigilant advance in single-file formation was the order of the day, with the lead scout taking the 'point' out front, followed by the Patrol Commander, or PC, and the Signaller, and the second-in-command, or 2IC, bringing up the rear as 'Tail-end Charlie'. The scout had the Owen sub-machine-gun, the PC had an SLR, and the other two men carried M1 carbines or Browning 12-gauge autoloader shotguns.

For the purposes of training, one four-man team would head into the jungle and make camp at a preselected RV, or rendezvous point. The second group then had to track them down. This they did with the aid of an experienced Iban tracker, who showed them what to look for by way of tell-tale signs such as broken twigs, faded footprints, or threads and cotton from drill fatigues that had been caught on branches when the first group, posing as the 'enemy', had passed by. The tracker also taught them how to magnetize a needle for use as a compass by rubbing it across a piece of silk and dangling it from a string, how to do the same with a razor blade by stropping it against the palm of the hand, and in general how to navigate in the jungle using the minimum of either natural or artificial aids.

Finally, although the men had already been trained in map-reading and the use of the standard-issue prismatic compass, they were taught how to judge distance in the jungle, how to use maps in relation to thick, impenetrable forest, how to use compass bearings and 'pacing' (counting the number of footsteps required) to reach a given destination, and how to take bearings and triangulate by means of the prismatic compass in daylight or darkness.

The Iban trackers came into their own with silent killing techniques and makeshift weapons. The SAS troopers had already been trained in various methods of the former, including martial-arts blows to the heart, lungs, liver, larynx, subclavian artery and spinal column and, of course, the cutting of the jugular vein with a knife. The trackers, however, showed them how to make spears by binding a knife to a 3-foot staff, shape a spear-thrower from a tree limb, make a compound bow and improvise weapons such as a sharpened wooden stake, a bone knife, a sock filled with soil and a garrotte made with two short wooden handles attached one to each end of a length of razor wire.

'Cut your fucking head clean off, that would,' Dennis the Menace said.

'They say a severed head remains conscious for up to twenty seconds after being lopped off,' Dead-eye solemnly informed them.

'My worst nightmare,' Boney Maronie said, 'is the twenty seconds of conversation I'd get after I'd garrotted Dennis. One second is bad enough.'

Back in the camp they had learnt special jungle preventative medicine from Royal Army Medical

Corps medics, but now, in the jungle, the aboriginals showed them many improvised medical techniques; these included cleaning wounds with urine (an extremely sterile liquid) where hot water is not available; packing infected wounds with maggots, which will eat only the 'dead' tissue; removing worms from the system by swallowing a small amount of petrol or kerosene; suturing severe cuts with needle and thread, making each suture individually; and improvising a splint with sticks rolled in cloth, a stretcher from tree branches rolled in blankets, or a jungle 'litter', or dangling stretcher, from bamboo or saplings bound together with creepers and suspended beneath a long pole. They also learned to improvise a tourniquet by wrapping a cloth three times around the limb, tying it with a half knot, placing a stick over the knot and securing it with a double knot, then twisting the stick until the cloth tightened enough to stop the bleeding.

Once they had mastered these jungle survival skills, the troopers, already worked to near exhaustion by daily practice on the firing range, were kept in the jungle to learn specialist jungle fighting tactics, such as ambush fire-control procedures, contact drills, fire and movement when breaking contact (or 'shoot and scoot') and firing at close range or in darkness.

When they emerged from the jungle they had all lost weight but gained an awful lot of knowledge.

Returning to the base, the men underwent the most frightening part of their training: tree-jumping, or parachuting into dense jungle, where the canopy was in some cases 150 feet high. Though this technique had not actually been tried before, the instructors were aware of three specific dangers: when a man crashed into the treetops, his parachute could snag, he could be smashed into thick branches or he could plummet through to the dense scrub below. As even the instructors had no experience to help them deal with such eventualities, they could do no more than remind the troopers to stay calm and use their common sense.

The training began with a static-line course which focused on the ground work, learning to deal with any problems that might arise during freefall and landing – for example, what to do if the soldier's 130lb of equipment sent him into an uncontrollable spin, or how to disentangle a parachute caught in branches. These lessons were followed by experimental climbs into the treetops while carrying 100 feet of rope, knotted every 18 inches. They would then tie one end of the rope to the canopy, let the other end fall to the ground, up to 150 feet below, and lower themselves by abseiling down the knotted rope. The stomach-churning climbs were followed by a series of experimental freefall jumps, carrying a rifle and a bergen strapped below the parachute, from a variety of aircraft into thinly wooded areas, leaving the aircraft at an altitude of 30,000 feet and opening the chute at 2,500 feet.

As High Altitude Low Opening (HALO) jumps into densely wooded areas had never been done before, even the parachute instructors could not help, so this phase of the training was ignored. Nevertheless, by the end of the extensive static-line training and fifty freefall jumps, some from high altitudes, others from dangerously low altitudes, the men were as prepared as they were ever likely to be.

'When do we do some *real* work?' Dennis the Menace asked.

'Tomorrow,' Sergeant Lorrimer replied.

5

'Ah Hoi's CTs are trying to grow food in a clearing in the Belum Valley, near the Thai border,' Major Pryce-Jones informed the men at the briefing that took place just after first light, 'and our job is to advance on that clearing and take out the guerrillas.'

'The real world at last!' Dennis the Menace said.

'Gurkhas, Royal Marine Commandos, Malaya Police and two squadrons of SAS are already approaching the site on foot,' Pryce-Jones continued as if he hadn't heard Dennis, though he threw a quick grin to Captain Callaghan, who was sitting in a chair to the side, smoking a cigarette. 'While they're doing so, you men will parachute into a confined DZ near the area and advance to the RV from there. The DZ will have been previously located and marked by Auster light observation aircraft flown by the Army Air Corps. It has to be assumed that when you parachute down, some of you will land in the trees. In such an event, we're hoping that the canopies will snag the branches firmly enough to belay you safely. With this in mind, you'll each be given, apart from your weapons, 100 feet of rope and some sound advice about tying knots.'

'Should have joined the bloody Navy!' Boney Maronie exclaimed to hoots of laughter.

'Don't forget, however,' Pryce-Jones continued when the laughter had died away, 'that if you land in bamboo it'll splinter and cut you to pieces. Also rocky areas, or spiky and weakened trees, can break bones and necks. In other words, when you're parachuting down, keep your eye on the treetops and manoeuvre away from anything too tricky. You'll embark on the march to the RV when you're all on the ground.'

'How long's the march, boss?' Dead-eye asked.

'That depends entirely on the terrain, which can't be gauged accurately from aerial photos. I'd estimate anything from a few days to a fortnight and either way you're in for a rough time. You'll have to hack your way through the undergrowth. You might find your way blocked by swamps. The rains can be so heavy they'll practically wash you away. Even in good weather, the *ulu* canopy is so thick that little light reaches the jungle floor and visibility is rarely more than fifty metres. Also, no matter how tough you are, you may find yourselves having to overcome a natural fear of the jungle environment, which is claustrophobic in the extreme and can cause severe lethargy. Even if you avoid that, you'll find that movement in the *ulu* is agonizingly slow and dangerous. Last but not least, enemy ambushes are likely to be mounted along rails and on crossing-points, which means you'll always have to opt for the more obscure, therefore more difficult and dangerous route. Given all these negative factors, it's an unpredictable scenario.'

'What about supplies?' Pete Welsh asked.

'Well, 55 Company Royal Army Service Corps are normally responsible for despatching supply containers to the ground forces from RAF aircraft, but as they've so far lost over a hundred men – killed when their planes crashed into the jungle – it's evident that resups aren't always easy to deliver in this environment. If absolutely necessary, resups will be dropped by Blackburn Beverleys or Valettas, but even when the planes manage to make their drops, the stores and equipment often becomes trapped high up on the jungle canopy, and have to be carried down by the troops on the ground, which merely makes for an additional hazard and a lot of wasted time. Therefore, for this operation we're introducing a special seven-to-fourteen-day patrol ration, so that you can operate for up to two weeks without resups.'

'What happens when we reach the RV?' Dead-eye asked in his usual serious manner. 'Do we take them out or hold them?'

'I'd rather have them alive than dead,' Pryce-Jones replied. 'The "green slime" can make use of them for intelligence purposes, then we can possibly convert them. On the other hand, the main purpose of the mission is to take them out and destroy their crops. How you do that will be decided on the spot by your Squadron Commander, Captain Callaghan. Any more questions?'

'Yes, boss,' Alf Laughton said. 'Since we've been deprived of our weekend in Penang, is there any chance of finding a decent bit of skirt in the jungle?'

Pryce-Jones answered the question dead-pan: 'In fact, a lot of the guerrillas are women and many of them are very attractive. But they all carry knives, know how to use them, and are quick to do so – particularly on the throats of "white devils". Any *more* questions?'

Everyone glanced at everyone else, but no one ventured another question. Taking note of their silence, Callaghan pushed his chair back and stood up, saying, 'Excellent. As you're all free of doubts or regrets, let's go and get kitted out.'

'Good luck,' Major Pryce-Jones said as the fifty-four men stood up and started out of the briefing room. He then nodded at Captain Callaghan, who nodded in turn at Sergeant Lorrimer.

'I'll follow you in a short while,' Callaghan said. 'Meanwhile, take care of them.'

'Right, boss,' Lorrimer said, then followed the other men out of the briefing room.

'Well, lads,' he heard Dennis the Menace say up ahead, as the men were crossing the sunny green field that led to the quartermaster's stores and armoury, 'that was an encouraging little briefing, was it not? Cut to pieces by bamboo, broken bones and necks, dense undergrowth, swamps and rain, no light, claustrophobia, and ambushes by female CT who cut white throats for breakfast. The boss sure knows how to cheer his men up!'

'Didn't bother me none,' said Pete Welsh, grinning crazily. 'I can take anything that's thrown at me. No sweat on *this* brow, mate!'

'You're sweating,' Alf Laughton told him. 'I can see you fucking sweating. It's pouring down your face like jungle rain. We can *all* see it, can't we, boys?'

'Yeah!' two or three chimed in.

'That's the heat,' Welsh shot back, still beaming. 'It's not a racing heart.'

'You don't have a fucking heart,' Dennis the

Menace said, 'so I suppose we've gotta believe you.'

The bullshit continued until they reached the quartermaster's stores, which was in a concrete block that included the armoury and radio store, all surrounded by papaya palms and neat hedgerows. The men were already wearing their rubber-and-canvas boots and special olive-green (OG) shirt and trousers, the former with long sleeves and manu-factured from cellular-weave cotton, the latter of a heavy-duty cotton. The full-length tails of the shirt and high waist of the trousers were designed, when combined, as protection from the *ulu's* numerous disease-carrying insects and leeches, as well as from the sharp spikes and edges of rattan, bamboo and palms, which could inflict serious wounds on bare skin. The only extra item of clothing required, therefore, was a soft green bush hat, to be worn in place of the beige beret.

As they had also already been supplied with their *parangs* and personal weapons, their main purpose at the quartermaster's stores was to pick up, along with the usual kit, special waterproof jungle bergens, cosmetic camouflage cream, dulling paint and strips of camouflage cloth for their weap-ons, lengths of para-cord to replace their weapons' standard-issue sling swivels, a plentiful supply of Paludrine, salt tablets, sterilization tablets, and a

Millbank bag, the latter being a canvas container used to filter collected water, which was then sterilized with the tablets.

'I'd be careful if I was you,' Dennis the Menace said helpfully to Boney Maronie as he packed his supply of tablets into a side-pocket of the bergen. 'These tablets are a con. They're actually filled with bromide. They don't stop the shits or sterilize water; they just deaden the sexual impulse, which the Ruperts think makes for a better soldier – one not distracted by thoughts of tit and arse. By the time you come out of that jungle, you won't know what a hard-on is.'

'Ha, ha, very funny,' Boney Maronie responded, trying to look unconcerned, though he couldn't help staring at the boxes of tablets in a questioning manner.

'What the fuck are you doing, Trooper?' Sergeant Lorrimer bawled at him. 'Are you in a trance there? Get on with your packing!'

'Yes, boss!' Boney Maronie snapped and got on with his packing as Dennis the Menace cackled beside him.

From the quartermaster's stores they marched the few yards to the armoury, where, since they already had their personal weapons, they picked up additional fire-power, including light machine-guns, mortars, fragmentation and smoke grenades, magazines of tracer bullets (to identify enemy positions in a fire-fight), flares, a couple of crossbows with lightweight alloy bolts and arrows, used for silent killing, and even some air rifles that fired darts which, though unlikely to kill, could cause painful minor wounds.

'Robin Hood and his Merry Men,' Boney Maronie said, inspecting the crossbow, which would be in his charge. 'It makes me feel like a kid again.'

'The guy who gets one of those bolts through him won't feel like a kid,' Dead-eye said. 'He'll feel a lot more than that.'

'If *you* fire it,' Dennis the Menace said, 'he won't feel a damned thing. He'll be dead in a second.'

'True enough,' Dead-eye said.

To their impressive collection of personal rifles they added the M16 assault rifle. Weighing only 3.72mg with a 30-round magazine, and fully automatic, it was able to put down a considerable amount of fire-power in a short space of time. Its main advantage, however, lay in its slightness, which enabled each member of the patrol to carry more ammunition. Also, it had a diverse range of attachments: a bayonet for close-quarters combat; a bipod for accuracy when firing from the prone position over longer ranges; and telescopic sights and night-vision aids. The M16 could also be fitted with an M203 40mm grenade-launcher, attached beneath the stock extending under the barrel, with a separate trigger mechanism forward of the magazine, capable of firing a variety of 40mm grenades including smoke, high-explosive (HE) and phosphorus, to a maximum accurate range of just under 40m.

Also picked up were a couple of L4A4 Bren guns with curved, 300-round box magazines of .303in bullets raised on the top, a swivel-down bipod located under the barrel, a mounting pin for use with a tripod, a pistol grip just behind the trigger and a carrying handle.

'I've fond memories of this little beauty,' Sergeant Lorrimer said, inspecting one of the L4A4s. 'It was a weapon much appreciated by the Maquis during World War Two. We also used it a lot in Africa, when with the Long Range Desert Group. Simple, old-fashioned and reliable.'

'Just like you, Sarge,' Boney Maronie quipped.

Lorrimer sighed. 'Yes, I suppose so.'

When all the weapons had been collected, the men moved along to the radio store, where they signed for their Clansman High-Frequency (HF) radio sets, one for each of the four-man teams. More commonly known as the PRC 320, the radio had dipoles, or horizontal antennae, rather than vertical aerials, as the latter could disclose a troop's position to the enemy. When used by ground troops the sets operated on compact batteries, but as this was a deep-penetration operation, each patrol also carried a lightweight, hand-powered generator to recharge the batteries, should the need arise.

Although the PRC 320 had a voice/speech capability, it was also used as a Morse or continuous-wave (CW) transmitter through a headset, which made it undetectable by the enemy. When using a whip antenna, it had a maximum range of 100km (voice), but the range became virtually limitless when the set was operating on CW in the sky-wave mode, where the operator's signal literally bounced off the earth's atmosphere.

Finally, each man collected his relatively simple World War Two Irvin X-Type model parachute, which he had to strap immediately to his back, so that he could carry the packed bergens and weapons by hand.

'We've got so much gear here,' Pete Welsh said in disbelief, 'the fucking Beverley probably won't be able to lift off.'

'We should be so lucky,' Dennis the Menace said.

'Stop moaning like a bunch of geriatrics,' Sergeant Lorrimer said, 'and hump all that stuff back to the spider.'

'Yes, boss!' Boney Maronie said, setting a good

example by somehow managing to get all of his gear into his bear-like arms and heading off across the sunlit field.

The 'spider' is the eight-legged dormitory-style sleeping quarters used by the SAS back in Britain, but the term was often applied to barracks elsewhere. Now, as Boney Maronie marched towards the barracks, all the other men followed him.

Entering the building, which in fact did not have eight legs but consisted of one long room with opposite rows of steel-framed beds and lockers, they went to their respective bashas, where they packed their kit properly. When this was done, the men painted their weapons with quick-drying green camouflage paint, then wrapped them in the strips of cloth specially dyed to match the jungle background and disguise their distinctive shape, taking great care not to let the paint or strips of cloth interfere with the weapons' working parts or sights. After wrapping masking tape around the butts, pistol grips and top covers, they replaced the noisy sling swivels with para-cord, which made no sound at all.

With the weapons camouflaged, the men's last job was to camouflage themselves, applying the 'cam' cream and black 'stick' camouflage to the exposed areas of their skin, including the backs of their hands, wrists, ears and neck. The facial camouflage was applied in three stages: first dulling the features with a thin base coating diluted with water (they would use their own saliva when in the jungle); then making diagonal patterns across the face to break up the shape and outline of the features; finally darkening the areas normally highlit, such as forehead, nose, cheek bones and chin. To complete this effect, areas normally in shadow were left a lighter shade.

When applying personal camouflage the patrol members paired off to check each other's appearance and ensure that nothing had been missed. This led, as usual, to a stream of bullshit.

'Do I look pretty?' Dennis the Menace asked.

'As sexy as a duck's arse,' Boney Maronie replied.

'If that were true, you'd be up me so fast my head would be spinning.'

'Give me a kiss, Dead-eye.'

'Knock it off, Pete.'

'When I see you with that eye-shadow, kid, I melt with love. Or at least I get an instant hard-on.'

'You should have worn a skirt and joined the WRAC. You'd be in good company there.'

'Oh, the kid has a tongue!'

'I wouldn't mess with him if I were you,' Alf Laughton said. 'That kid's sweet face is a mask for deadly talents. He's the kind to explode.'

'That he does every night,' Boney Maronie cut in, 'which is why his sheets are soaked in more than sweat.'

'Aw, knock it off!' Dead-eye exclaimed, his blushes hidden by the dark camouflage. 'Why don't you blokes be serious?'

Before anyone could reply, Sergeant Lorrimer appeared in the doorway to bawl: 'All right, you limp dicks! Are you ready?'

'Yes, boss!' came the reply from many voices.

'Then pick your kit up and let's go.'

Heavily burdened, the fifty-four men left the gloom of the spider and marched into the rising heat of the early morning. A couple of Bedford three-tonners had been driven across from the motor pool and were waiting outside, but before the men could board they were inspected personally by Captain Callaghan. Satisfied that everything was in order, he gave them permission to board the Bedfords. The trucks then transported them to the airstrip, where three Vickers Valetta twin-engine aircraft, known affectionately as 'flying pigs' because of their bulbous shape, were waiting to fly them into the interior. Almost as soon as the men and their equipment had been transferred from the Bedfords to the Valettas, the aircraft took off.

Wedged tightly together and hemmed in by their weapons, bergens and supplies, the men joked and laughed for a few minutes after take-off. Eventually, tired of having to shout against the steady roar of the Valettas' twin Bristol Hercules turboprops, they fell silent, each preparing himself in his own way for what was to come. Some slept, others read, a few chewed gum or ate fruit. A few glanced out of the windows, fixing their eyes on the jungle far below, wondering what it would be like to parachute down into what looked like an almost solid, vibrant-green canopy of densely packed treetops.

'Ten minutes to go!' the Army Air Corps Load-master called out, perhaps sounding so cheerful because he would not be one of those parachuting down into that deceptively lovely jungle.

The men checked each other's gear. Some were restless and checked it twice. Not knowing when they would get the chance to eat again, a couple of them ate hurried last-minute snacks of apples, oranges, or bananas. Few had bread or biscuits because already their throats were dry from the heat inside the plane and, as they knew, the humidity of the jungle would be even worse.

'Dropping Zone, two minutes to go,' the Load-master informed them. 'Your altitude is 225 metres.'

Sergeant Lorrimer was the first to stand up, placing himself where all the men could see and hear him. 'Two-twenty-five metres,' he repeated. 'That means you'll have less than a minute to spot and steer for a solid tree, so keep your wits about you.'

'Stand up!' the Loadmaster bawled, opening the large boom door and letting the slipstream roar in. 'Action stations!'

The men stood in two lines, to the left and right of the boom door. As the Irvin X-Type model parachute had to be opened by hand, they did not have to connect static lines to the plane.

The first man out was Sergeant Lorrimer, who was acting as 'drifter' to discover the strength and direction of the wind. Though the veteran of more than 100 descents, he was still wary of tree-jumping and nervous of the odds-on chance that he would find himself dangling in a treetop with broken limbs or, even worse, a fractured spine. First swept sideways in the slipstream in the combined roaring of the wind and the aircraft's engines, he suddenly fell vertically, popped the parachute, was jerked back up for a moment, then fell more gently as the chute billowed open above him like a great, white mushroom. In just under a minute the jungle canopy was rushing up towards him and he found himself spinning rapidly into a tree. But he was lucky: although his feet and body smashed into the branches, the chute caught and held him.

Lorrimer was dangling about 150 feet above the ground. All he could see through the branches and leaves was thick undergrowth. Above him, the Valetta, which had been circling until the pilot saw him land, began its first run in over the DZ. As the aircraft came towards him, Sergeant Lorrimer disentangled himself from the branches, unwound his knotted rope, tied one end to a secure branch, let the other fall, and began to lower himself to the ground.

Having checked the strength and direction of the wind from Lorrimer's descent, the pilot slightly altered the course of the Valetta to allow for a more accurate fall. Inside the plane, the green light flashed again above the door and the SAS paratroopers prepared to jump. They went out one by one, but in 'sticks' of three from the left and right of the large boom door, as the Loadmaster patted each of them on the shoulder, bawling: '*Right, right, right!*'

Standing in the doorway, even Dead-eye was nervous, though he knew there was no turning back now. So, when he felt the Loadmaster's tap on his shoulder and heard him bawl '*Right!*', he didn't hesitate. As he launched himself into the slipstream, there was a sudden roaring, and the breath was sucked from his lungs. The next thing he knew, he was floating down through the air,

looking first at the vast blue sweep of the sky, then
at the approaching sea of green jungle, and feeling
almost magically alive.

He was descending beautifully, steering for the
middle of the trees. Then a gust of hot air made
him swing violently, as if a giant had caught hold of
him and was shaking him. Remaining calm, he let
the air spill out of the chute and began to look for
a healthy tree. This he found impossible, however
– the jungle canopy was too dense – until he was
only a few feet above the canopy. By then it was
too late and he smashed into a tangle of treetops,
came to a brief halt, already feeling battered and
bruised, then heard the branch snapping and
suddenly hurtled down, crashing through more
branches and thinking he was being smashed to
pieces. He came to a shuddering halt, snared in
a lower branch, from which he wriggled free and
dropped the last few feet.

Already on the ground, Sergeant Lorrimer grinned
with contentment, but not everyone made it down
that easily. Swinging from the top of one tall tree,
as the last of the other parachutists descended
successfully, was Boney Maronie. Temporarily
paralysed with fear at being so high up, he tried
to disguise it by lighting a cigarette. He gave up
in this endeavour – his hands were shaking so
much he couldn't light it – and eventually, when

the last of the other parachutists had landed and everyone began to shout at him to come down, he fixed his knotted rope to the treetop, separated the parachute container from his bergen, secured the bergen to his shoulders, then abseiled down the tree on the knotted rope, dropping the last five or six feet in his desperate need to feel the ground beneath his feet.

'Spot of bother up there?' Sergeant Lorrimer asked him when the cheering and applause of the troopers had finally died down.

'Piece of piss,' Boney Maronie said. 'I was just having a rest.'

'Very wise,' Captain Callaghan said. 'OK, men, let's move out.'

They headed into the darkness of the jungle.

6

Captain Pryce-Jones had been right: the *ulu* closed in on them so fast that most of them suffered an initial claustrophobia and panic that had to be overcome. It was related to the extraordinary height of the trees, the seemingly solid nature of the canopy high above, the absence of light on the jungle floor, the dense, almost impenetrable undergrowth, the knowledge that poisonous snakes, centipedes and scorpions could fall on them from the overhanging foliage or crawl over their booted feet. Last but not least was the appalling humid heat, which instantly made all of the men sweat profusely and some of them feel almost suffocated.

As the Malayan jungle is evergreen, none of the varieties of trees sheds all its leaves at once, which explains the unusual density of the canopy and the gloomy, colourless nature of the jungle floor, which was covered in a thick carpet of dead leaves and seedlings, lying around the giant roots and thick creepers of the soaring trees, entwined with vines and lianas. The *ulu* is constantly rotting and regenerating, with ferns, mosses and herbaceous plants pushing through the leaves and fungi growing thickly on leaves and fallen tree trunks. Colouring the canopy, however, was a mass of white, yellow, pink, or scarlet blossom, often so sweetly scented that even the jungle far below was filled with the fragrance of the invisible flowers high above. This sickly-sweet smell made some of the men feel even more suffocated as they made their agonizingly slow advance.

The general feeling of tension was increased in other ways. As each man had been equipped with one magazine full of tracer bullets, which were to be used to identify enemy positions in a fire-fight, they were all uneasily conscious of the unseen enemy. Also, Captain Callaghan had made them place the magazines in their ammunition pouches upside down, with the bullets pointed away from the body in case they were hit by enemy fire and injured the wearer. Likewise, to ensure that they would not make good targets for the enemy, hand-grenades were not carried on the chest as they would have been in other environments. All of this simply served to highlight the nerve-racking fact that the enemy could be anywhere in the *ulu*, preparing an ambush.

Not allowed to talk or trade bullshit while on the march, forced to communicate only with hand signals, the troopers could not ignore the sounds of the jungle and therefore were prone to imagine things, which made for even more nervous tension.

In the daytime, the jungle was relatively quiet, but they would occasionally hear the hornbill, whose loud, discordant voice resembles that of a heron. They would also hear the rhythmic, noisy beating of its wings and, if there happened to be a break in the treetops, they would see its huge, black, ungainly form and its bizarrely shaped white head. It was the only living thing they had seen so far.

As the men would soon discover, the patrol would be on the move ten hours a day with only occasional breaks and brief halts. Their advance took them alternately from the humid swamp of the jungle to open river beds, where the harsh sun temporarily dried their sweat-soaked fatigues, but then baked their bodies and feet in fierce dry heat, which in some ways was even worse.

The burden of their weapons, radios, other items of equipment and supplies was a source of considerable frustration and led to a torrent of whispered obscenities. The weapons in particular were covered with knobs, swivels, handles, catches, guards and other protuberances which, however they were carried, scraped and bruised the hip bone, dug into the ribs and caught on every twig and creeper in the undergrowth, sometimes tugging the unwary owner practically off his feet.

Using a map in combination with aerial photographs of the terrain, Captain Callaghan managed to locate a watercourse that he hoped would provide a relatively easy route to a Sakai village, where he planned to pick up some guides. Unfortunately, when they reached the watercourse, they discovered that it was too deep and rough to follow easily, with sides so steep and so covered with bamboo, thorns and thickets of every kind that their progress was even slower than it had been in the jungle. To make matters even worse, where the ground of the watercourse was still wet, they found it almost impossible to keep their feet on the steep traverses and repeatedly, painfully tore their hands when clutching at twigs to prevent themselves from falling.

They camped that first evening on a sandbank several feet above the water-line, this being the only level place they could find. It was a relief in more ways than one, particularly as they could bathe, eat, drink and talk again, reasonably confident that the guards located far out on all four points would give them fair warning of any advancing enemy troops.

'The worst of all is not being able to talk,' Dennis the Menace said as he started stripping off his sweat-soaked clothing to dive naked into the river. 'When all you can listen to is this fucking jungle, you keep hearing things that aren't there.'

'You're a nutcase,' Boney Maronie said. 'I always knew it; now I've got solid proof.'

'There speaks the brave,' Dennis said. 'He was so scared on the top of that bloody tree, he almost shook the whole damned thing down.'

'Bullshit,' Boney Maronie retorted. 'I told you – I was just resting up until the latecomers landed on the DZ.'

'So how come you didn't light the cigarette that fell down from the treetops? The shakes, was it?'

'Fuck you, Dennis, I . . . *Shit*!' Stripped to the waist, Boney Maronie now saw what they were all suddenly noticing – that clusters of bloated leeches were stuck to various parts of their bodies. 'Jesus Christ!' Boney Maronie exclaimed in revulsion.

'Fucking hell,' chimed in Dennis the Menace, stripping off his OG trousers and standing in his pants to display a body completely covered in blood-sucking leeches. 'I've been pulling the bastards off me all day, so I didn't expect to find more. I'm being sucked dry!' He sat down again, lit a cigarette, inhaled and blew a cloud of smoke. 'Little fuckers!' he said, studying the glowing end of his cigarette.

Dead-eye Dick had also pulled off scores of leeches during the day and did not know that others had crawled through his clothing until he felt the blood running down his chest. Now, as he and his fellow troopers tried queasily to remove the bloodsuckers, Dennis the Menace started stubbing the end of his cigarette on to those clinging to his bared thighs, making them sizzle, smoke and shrivel up.

'God!' Pete West exclaimed, turning up his nose, 'that's bloody disgusting!'

'Disgusting to you,' Dennis the Menace said, 'but it makes sense to me. If you pull these little fuckers off, their teeth stay in and fester. Nope, you should only remove them by touching them with salt, tobacco, a solution of areca nut or a cigarette end.' To prove his point, he eagerly scorched another of the creatures.

'Aw, knock it off, Dennis!' Alf Laughton complained.

'It's the only sensible way, mate.'

'That's bullshit,' Boney Maronie said, wincing each time he pulled a leech off a bleeding wound. 'I've been told that removing leeches that way is no better than any other. The wounds bleed just as much and they're just as likely to become infected. Might as well just pull them off like this.' He pulled another insect off and winced again, putting on a brave show.

'Doesn't matter how you get rid of 'em,' Pete Welsh said, 'as long as you do it.' He, too, was smoking, touching his burning cigarette to the leeches on his body one by one, grinning dementedly as they sizzled. 'A lot of people have actually died from leeches – from the swelling that comes from their bites.'

'Crap,' Dead-eye said.

'It's bloody not. The wounds from leeches sometimes swell so much that they block the body's orifices and cause a slow, agonizing death.'

'What orifices?' Dead-eye asked sceptically.

'Lips, nostrils, arse-hole and the eye of your dick.'

'Ah, God!' Boney Maronie cried. 'Knock it off! I can't bear even thinking about that.'

Then, stripped completely naked and having nothing to hide, he jumped into the river.

Now naked as well, though not so keen to flaunt it, Dennis the Menace wrapped a towel around his waist, hurried to the river bank and tentatively waded in.

'What was that dangling between your legs?'

Boney Maronie asked when he surfaced. 'Another leech, was it?'

'Go fuck yourself,' Dennis the Menace said, sinking gratefully chest-deep in the water, soon followed by Dead-eye, Pete Welsh, Alf Laughton and an increasing number of the other men, all desperately grateful to have the sweat and the blood of the many leeches washed off them.

As the men were stopping at this location for only one night, they did not make up proper shelters, just personal Laying Up Positions, or LUPs, consisting mainly of uncovered shallow 'scrapes' in which they unrolled their hollow-fill sleeping bags on plastic sheeting. Above these simple beds they raised a shelter consisting of a waterproof poncho draped over wiring stretched taut between two Y-shaped sticks, making a triangular shape with the apex pointing into the wind.

Reasonably sure that there were no CT in the vicinity, and knowing that the camp was being guarded on all sides, they were confident enough to prepare hot food with the aid of portable hexamine stoves, followed by a much-appreciated brew-up and, for many, a 'smoko'.

As clothes saturated with sweat would quickly rot, Callaghan ordered some of the men to make a 'trench fire'. This they did by digging a trench about a foot deep, lining the bottom with rocks and stones from the river and lighting a fire of sticks and hexamine blocks on top of the rocks. As the flames were protected from any wind and could not set the surrounding foliage alight, the trench fire was ideal for drying out the troopers' soaked fatigues.

'We should raise these bashas off the ground,' Dead-eye said, 'to make sure the spiders, scorpions, centipedes and snakes don't get at us.'

'Oh, thanks very much,' Dennis the Menace said, as he unrolled his sleeping bag, 'for giving us all something to think about when we try to get some shut-eye.'

'I only meant . . .'

'I know what you mean and I know you're right, but I still don't want to hear it, kid,' the older man interrupted. 'We can't raise the bashas off the ground without building platforms of bamboo and thatch, but that's too much work for this short time. So here we are and here we stay for the night. Don't give us bad dreams, Dead-eye.'

Nevertheless, knowing that the creepy-crawlies were more likely to be drawn to dry clothing and footwear, they quickly constructed a simple raised platform by weaving elephant grass and palm leaves through cross-pieces of branches supported on four lengths of split bamboo. They piled their dried clothing and jungle boots up on the platform, which had been constructed, for additional protection, near the all-night trench fire.

'That takes care of the clothes and boots,' Dead-eye said, not concerned about the guerrillas, though he was clearly still wary of insects. 'But what about us?'

'Smear yourself with mud from the river,' Sergeant Lorrimer told him and the others, 'then cover your sleeping bags with leaves. You should all have sweet dreams.'

This they did, but it meant that they would have to sleep without moving much, which ensured that sleep did not come easily. There was another bar to sleeping. As darkness closed in, the jungle chorus, which had been hushed during the day, came to life and built up in an almost deafening crescendo, with every imaginable species of grasshopper, cicada and tree frog competing in a musical, rhythmic, discordant, cacophonous medley. Some sounded like alarm clocks, others like tinkling bells, yet others like hunting horns, a few like distant pneumatic drills. There were yodelling, clicking, gargling and rattling sounds and, worst of all, a pervasive humming that sounded like millions of insects imprisoned and going frantic in glass jars.

By night, the jungle was a symphony that could drive a man mad.

It was at night, too, that the insects ruled over their own domain. In the daytime, they did not trouble the men too much, but at night they were insatiable, driven frantic by the need for the salt in human sweat, relentlessly whining around the men's ears and biting them constantly, no matter how much they were slapped away.

Even worse than the mosquitoes were the midges, which made no noise but gave a bite that itched like a nettle sting and kept the victim awake throughout the night.

As a result of the many bites they received in the night, the men's faces in the morning were so swollen and distorted that they were, in many cases, almost unrecognizable. Indeed, some had cheeks so swollen that their eyes were closed and they couldn't see until they bathed them in cold water.

For most of the men, that first night was one of the worst they had ever experienced. Nevertheless, they moved out the next day – only to find it even more difficult than the first.

In the depths of the jungle, the limit of visibility was reduced to between 50 and 100 yards. Even when they were on a steep hillside, where a small landslide had opened up a window through which they could catch a glimpse of another tree-covered hillside, surmounted by sheer blue sky, they were none the wiser about their whereabouts, one hill looking exactly like another. There were no landmarks – and even if there were, they could not be seen. Another difficulty was that the scouts, or point men, had no way of judging distance: it took them three days to realize they were taking eight hours to travel one mile on the map instead of the three or four miles they had imagined, judging by the amounts of energy they were expending. Also, they were continually forced off their course by swamps, thickets, precipices, outcrops of rock and rivers. It was impossible even to follow a ridge unless it was very steep and clearly marked.

Sometimes they clambered up hills so steep that they had to hold on to the vegetation with both hands to pull themselves up, and on the descents had to lower themselves carefully from branch to branch. On such arduous climbs and descents they met every kind of prickly thicket, and sometimes came across rhododendron, coarse shrubs and moss so thick that they clambered over the top of them without actually touching the ground.

The worst going of all, however, consisted of whole valleys filled with huge granite boulders half-covered with a slippery layer of moss and with treacherous roots, so that a false step was liable to land them in the stream below. Their bergens seemed to get heavier and heavier; their weapons, snagging everything, became close to unbearable.

Even worse was the number of times the lead man, unless carefully watched, would turn through half a circle in a few minutes without being in the least aware of it, as he could not see the sun and there were no landmarks, apart from the interminable tree trunks, from which to take his bearings. When Captain Callaghan realized this was happening, he devised a new system.

'In future the man at the front won't carry his Owen sub-machine-gun. Instead, he'll use his *parang* to cut a path that he can pass through, even if just about. The second man will then widen the track and mark the route more clearly by bending saplings down or blazing tree trunks, and the third man will then follow through and check the course with a compass.'

'That sounds like hell for the first man,' Sergeant Lorrimer said.

'It will be,' Callaghan replied. 'For that very reason, the men will change places every half hour.'

The new approach worked well, though it exhausted the men hacking their way through the undergrowth and there were many minor wounds because of their inexperience with the razor-sharp *parang*, even after their training in Johore. Nevertheless, it hastened their advance and so they stuck to it. They were grateful, however, when, after four days on the march, they finally reached a Sakai village, where a couple of the aboriginals, known to Captain Callaghan, agreed to act as their guides to the RV.

'That's a relief,' Callaghan said to Lorrimer as they sat in the shade of one of the raised thatched huts, enjoying a brew-up and a cigarette. 'We seem to be taking longer every day, so I'm glad the Sakai are on board at last.'

'Bloody amazing, isn't it?' Lorrimer replied. 'You do all that training back at base, but once you're in the actual jungle, most of the training comes to nought. The *ulu* is so damned unpredictable.'

'Well, not *all* of the training comes to nought, Sarge. In fact, most of it holds up very well, if these men are anything to judge by. They've adapted remarkably quickly, when all's said and done. They've endured an awful lot in four days.'

'That's true enough. Even you, I suppose, couldn't have survived three months on your own if it hadn't been for your special jungle training.'

'No. I'll be eternally grateful for it.'

'You weren't so grateful when I was one of the directing staff.'

Callaghan chuckled at his recollection of Sergeant Lorrimer as a particularly ruthless DS during his personal training course in Johore. 'God, you were tyrannical, Sarge! A real bloody monster.'

'The proof is in the pudding,' Lorrimer said.

'I take that as a compliment.'

They moved out shortly after, this time with the Sakai guides out front, instead of SAS point men. Nevertheless, the hike through the jungle was no easier and, at times, even worse.

Every evening, when they stopped to make camp, the men de-leeched themselves and washed away the clotted blood. Then, as the noisy, biting insects became intolerable, they made a fresh leaf-shelter for the night. They soon became adept at this. Usually, they made a low framework with a sloping roof and lashed it firmly in place with vines. After collecting the largest leaves available, they thatched them into the framework of the roof. They then made a huge pile of branches and leaves as a mattress, put on all their clothes, smeared themselves with mud, if available, and finally covered themselves with groundsheets.

'I'm actually getting used to this,' Dennis the Menace said. 'Last night I almost had a whole night's sleep.'

'You still woke up looking like Bela Lugosi,' Boney Maronie said, laughing. 'Your face was bitten all to hell and your eyes were puffed up.'

'That's how he looks every morning,' Pete Welsh

said, 'even back in Blighty. That's why his wife ran away with the milkman.'

'How did you know that?' Dennis the Menace replied. 'I never told a soul about it.'

'Pete was the milkman,' Boney Maronie said.

'Seriously, though, lads,' Dennis the Menace said, 'it's amazing how you can learn to be comfortable even in these conditions – smeared with mud and covered with leaves and shrubbery. I'm almost getting to like it.'

'The mud helps a bit,' Alf Laughton said. 'At least the midges bite less. But it doesn't kill the whining of those fucking mosquitoes. I think they go even more frantic when they can't get at your bare skin. Their whining drives me insane.'

'Really?' Boney Maronie said. 'I hadn't noticed. You haven't changed at all, Alf.'

'Go and screw yourself, Boney!'

'Real cosy in here,' Dennis the Menace said, practically purring. 'I know I'm in for a good night.'

The rain came. It poured down like a waterfall. Though they had been told that bamboo always burns, no matter how wet, they learnt the hard way that this is true only when the fire is already burning. Thus, when the rain came unexpectedly – as it did – they could neither start a fire nor burn the hexamine stoves, and so were not only drenched, but had to eat cold tinned rations instead of hot food. It was a fierce, noisy tropical cloudburst that almost washed them away.

'Fucking hell!' Boney Maronie exclaimed as he huddled up beside Dennis the Menace, both wrapped in their ponchos. 'This is bloody terrible.'

'Noah's Ark should pass by any minute now.'

'I'm soaked to the bloody skin.'

'So am I. Even the leeches are drowning.'

'It's so noisy!' Dead-eye exclaimed, his voice muffled by the poncho covering his face. 'It sounds like jungle drums.'

'I hate this kind of racket,' Pete Welsh said. 'It gets on my nerves.'

'Tropical rains don't last long,' Alf Laughton said, 'so this should stop pretty soon.'

He was wrong. In fact, the rain was merely the prelude to the violent gale known as *Sumatras* – a terrifying experience that began as a loud roaring in the distance, but gradually increased in volume until it sounded like a squadron of fighter aircraft flying overhead.

In fact, thinking it was an air raid, some of the men instinctively dived for cover, including Dennis the Menace, Boney Maronie and Dead-eye. Face down in the mud, they soon realized that they were wrong – they weren't hearing aircraft, but something much worse. Sitting up again, they squinted into the rain and saw, through a narrow window in the rain-lashed, wind-blown trees, a boiling mass of black clouds streaked by jagged fingers of lightning. The roaring sound was a fearsome combination of thunder and wind.

'Shit,' Boney Maronie whispered, 'that wind is fierce!'

'*Sumatras*!' the Sakai guide nearby exclaimed in a hoarse, frightened whisper.

'*Take cover*!' Captain Callaghan bawled, before disappearing behind an enormous tree.

The storm exploded over them with awesome force, tearing the trees to shreds, filling the air with flying debris, picking some of the men up and flinging them back down like rag dolls. The noise was terrifying, and bolts of lightning daggered down into the forest like crooked fingers of silvery fire. The wind hurled the rain before it, turning it into a deluge, creating a whirlpool filled with flying foliage, including sharp-edged palms that slashed like razors across the upraised arms and hands of some of the men. They were screaming with pain even as a couple of trees toppled over, crashing down through the other trees, tearing the great branches off, creating a torrent of branches, vines, lianas, creepers and giant leaves, which rained down to add their own noise to the bedlam.

Far louder, great trees smashed down through smaller ones and crashed into the forest floor, right across the path of the patrol. Then the storm passed on as quickly as it had arrived, leaving an eerie silence.

When eventually the men crawled out of where they had been hiding, the first thing they saw, among the piled-up and widely strewn debris, was the decapitated head of one of the Sakai guides. What was left of his body was buried deep in the mud under the fallen truck of a giant tree.

'We'll never be able to dig him out,' Captain Callaghan said, 'so just bury his head.'

While most of the men looked on, hardly believing what they were seeing, the remaining Sakai guides buried the head, then held a funeral ceremony around the small mound of earth, all of them bowed low in prayer as the sodden trees dripped over their already soaked bodies.

First bogged down by the storm, then, when it abated, by the sea of mud, fallen trees and scattered foliage of its aftermath, the men took a long time in pulling themselves together. Nevertheless, hearing over the PRC 320 that the foot patrols consisting of Gurkhas, Royal Marine Commandos, Malaya Police and two squadrons of SAS were nearing the

RV, they were encouraged enough to move on into the drying, steaming jungle.

Their damaged morale was not boosted when one of the troopers complained of a terrible pain behind his eyes, aching in all his joints and alternating spasms of fever and freezing cold. When examined by the doctor, he was found to be running a temperature of 103 degrees and was diagnosed as suffering from benign tertiary – a virulent, though not serious, form of malaria.

A few hours later, the doctor was called upon to attend a trooper who had contracted blackwater fever, brought on when he had developed chronic malaria and failed to take enough quinine to combat it. As well as the symptom from which the disease derives its name, the trooper suffered relentless vomiting and dysentery, accompanied by such agonizing pains in the small of his back and across his pelvis that he complained about feeling as if all his bones were coming apart. Eventually, he had to be held down by two other troopers to counteract the violence of the spasms. After these had subsided, he was rolled on to a makeshift stretcher and carried the rest of the way.

The storm having blown itself out, the men moved on and found themselves facing a series of parallel rivers, which they crossed on bamboo rafts quickly built with the help of the Sakai.

Four feet wide and 30 feet long, the rafts were made by lashing together a double layer of 4-inch bamboos. The central third was raised by lashing on an additional deck of shorter poles, and the load was placed there, amidships, where it kept comparatively dry. As soon as it was light enough to see the feathery bamboo groves overhanging the bank, the men started poling the raft down-river to the RV, now only a few miles away.

As they travelled down the river, between high banks of mud and papaya trees, they learnt over the PRC 320 that the foot patrols, which had been marching for seven days, had finally reached Ah Hoi's jungle hide-out – only to discover that the guerrilla chief had fled with his men and the camp was empty.

'They must have been warned of our approach by the Communist agents in the villages along the route,' SAS Captain Tony Lidgate explained over the radio.

'We haven't spotted any CT either,' a disappointed Captain Callaghan informed him. 'Not one. Not a shadow.'

'They must have spotted the Valetta circling over the DZ,' Lidgate said.

Callaghan sighed, glancing around him at the exhausted men squatting on the raft. 'We can destroy the camp and farm,' he said, 'but it seems like a great deal of effort for such a small gain. A damned waste of time, in fact.'

'Not necessarily. We've just been in contact with Johore and been informed by the CO that we're to remain in the CT camp and turn it into a Forward Operating Base.'

'A good idea,' Captain Callaghan said, feeling the return of enthusiasm. 'An FOB in that location could be invaluable.'

'We're settling in already,' Lidgate said, 'and should have the tea on the brew by the time you get here. I'll see you then, Captain. Over and out.'

Callaghan switched the microphone off and handed it back to the radio operative, then he looked along the river to where it curved away between green walls of undergrowth and soaring trees. When the rafts turned that bend in the river, they saw the thatched huts and lean-tos of the abandoned CT camp, now filled with Gurkhas, Royal Marine Commandos, Malaya Police, Sakai and Iban trackers, and the two squadrons of SAS troopers.

'Home sweet home,' Captain Callaghan murmured, grinning at Sergeant Lorrimer as the rafts were poled to the shore.

7

When the men were at last resting gratefully on thatched mats in the shade of the lean-tos, some eating, some having a brew-up, others urgently cleaning themselves and shaving with the aid of hand mirrors, they were astonished to discover how much weight they had lost in a mere five days in the jungle. In fact, their bones stuck out everywhere and their skin, except where it was mottled with the purple spots of hundreds of leech bites, was a sickly yellow. Their clothes were in ragged tatters, and their hands, knees and faces were covered with a network of cuts and thorn scratches, as well as the larger cuts inflicted upon some by flying sharp-edged leaves during the terrifying *Sumatras*. The Royal Marine Commandos, Malaya Police and other two squadrons of SAS troopers did not look much better, though the Gurkhas, Sakai and Iban trackers looked much as usual.

Not far from where some of the men were resting, at the edge of the jungle just beyond the perimeter of the camp, a gibbon – a *wah-wah* in Malay – was swinging from branch to branch with its long arms.

'That,' Alf Laughton said, 'is the only animal we've seen throughout the whole march. Considering the jungle's supposed to be full of them, I think that's bloody amazing.'

'Well, I'm bloody amazed,' Pete Welsh said sarcastically.

While the men were resting up, Captain Callaghan exchanged reports with the other squadron commander, Captain Lidgate, then used the PRC 320 to contact Johore and arrange for supplies to be dropped. Later that afternoon, these were dropped by parachute from a Blackburn Beverley, which, with its payload capacity of 20,500kg, was able to deliver a substantial amount.

After their lengthy hike, or 'tab', through the jungle, the men were allowed to rest for most of the day. However, once the Beverley had flown overhead, their rest period ended and they were sent off in various directions to bring in the supplies that had fallen both in and outside the camp. When they had done this, stacking the supplies up in the middle of the compound, they were allocated various small tasks that would see them through the first night in some comfort: first washing themselves in the river, then the construction of trench fires for the cooking of some decent food, then a late-evening dinner, followed by beer and a smoko, and finally the preparation of temporary bashas.

Early next morning, however, they all took part in the construction of a proper FOB.

The guerrillas' camp had consisted of not much more than a few thatched lean-tos scattered around the clearing near open trenches filled with human excrement, urine and many thousands of seething, stinking maggots. The SAS plan was to construct a fully circular base camp surrounded by a cleared track, hemmed in with wire, and protected by Claymore mines and sentry posts.

First, though, they had to get rid of the maggots, which were giving even the most hardened troopers the shivers. They disposed of them by pouring kerosene into the trenches and setting light to it, creating half-a-dozen bonfires. While the bonfires burned, the rest of the work began in earnest.

As it was vitally important that the FOB could be defended by a fraction of the men while the majority of them were on patrol, the camp was designed within a circular cleared track that divided it from the surrounding jungle. This track, dug out of the ground over several days by SAS troopers with shovels and spades, formed an 'open' area that would have to be crossed by anyone, friend or enemy, wanting to enter the camp.

As some of the troopers were clearing the track, others were digging a series of defensive slit trenches at regular intervals around the camp, on the inner side of the circle, to be used as permanent sentry positions that would face out in every direction. The defensive trenches were similar to rectangular observation posts, or OPs, in that they had room for at least four men and shallow 'resting up' scrapes. However, unlike long-term OPs, they were open to the air.

At the same time, other trenches were being dug out in a smaller circle near the centre of the compound where the Sakai were constructing a large headquarters, which would be surrounded by similar constructions to be used as living quarters, cookhouse, mess hall, stores, and even a small area for football and general exercise. As the camp would have no vehicles, there was no need for a motor pool, but a helicopter landing pad was being levelled in the south-east corner of the circular compound.

The Sakai were expert at constructing the buildings and did so with the aid of curious SAS troopers. The framework of each building was made from poles of green timber, 6 inches in diameter. The stronger timber from standing trees was used to support the main beam of the roof. As most of the Sakai were expert axemen, they felled and trimmed the poles while the SAS troopers went out collecting the rattan required to bind the joints.

The rattan is a creeper that can grow to hundreds of feet in length, coiling along the ground before climbing to the summit of the tallest trees, where it bursts into a huge umbrella of giant leaves. Some rattan are two inches thick, but the ideal thickness for jungle constructions is one-third to half an inch. When one of suitable size was found, two or three troopers would pull it out of the ground or down from the trees. As the jointed green cane of the rattan is protected by a thorny shell, this would be stripped off, then the pliable stem would be coiled up like a rope and carried back to the Sakai in charge of the construction. Using a small, sharp knife, the Sakai would then split each rattan into two separate parts or, for finer lashings, into strips, then he would cut away and discard the inner pith.

While some of the Sakai were building the framework of the huts or splitting the rattan, others were teaching the SAS troopers to plait *atap* for the roofing material. Large clumps of *atap* were to be found near by, with drooping fronds 20–30 feet long. The fronds were pulled down with a crook and the top 8 feet of the pithy stalk cut off, stacked in special racks to prevent the leaves being damaged, then carried back to the camp in bundles. To plait the *atap*, all the leaves on one side starting at the base had to be bent back sharply, then threaded under and over the leaves on the other side of the central stem, thus giving a plaited surface 6–8 inches wide.

The *atap* was placed horizontally on the framework of the roof, starting at the bottom. It was then lashed in two places with fine rattan to the vertical members of the roof, which had been cut from the lower stems of *atap*. The *atap* was placed so that every part of the roof was covered by about eight thicknesses of plaited leaf, presenting on the outside an even surface of downwards-pointing leaf ends. At the apex of the roof a number of plaited *atap* were laid along the join of the two sides and pegged beneath the roof beam. The gables of the huts were filled in with *atap*, forming an unbroken surface, with the sides and ends left entirely open.

As for the bashas, where the SAS men slept, an aisle about 6 feet wide was left down the centre of each hut, with the timber-framed beds, or sleeping-benches, on either side raised about a couple of feet off the ground. The beds themselves consisted of elephant grass and palm leaves woven through cross-pieces of branches supported on pieces of split bamboo. Some of the troopers were able to sleep comfortably on these; others rolled their sleeping bag out and used it as a mattress.

All the buildings were raised off the ground on stilts to lessen the chance of invasion by poisonous snakes, centipedes, scorpions and giant jungle rats.

When the fires in the latrine trenches had stopped burning, thatched lean-tos were raised over the separate latrines, with bamboo walls between each, thus granting a modicum of privacy to the users. The trenches were filled with a mixture of quicklime and kerosene to prevent the return of the hideous maggots.

By this time the cleared path around the compound had been completed and was lined with a barbed-wire fence in which there were two openings, one as a Patrol Route Entry, the other as a Patrol Route Exit. The defensive trenches spaced at regular intervals around the inner side of the fence were manned permanently by SAS teams with tripod-mounted Bren guns and 3-inch mortars.

Claymore mines were laid around the camp, just outside the perimeter, on the other side of the cleared path, except for the areas directly facing both the Patrol Route Entrance and Exit. Set to be activated manually, or when someone stepped on them, they were shaped like concave plates which, on exploding, would fire around 350 metal balls over a fan-shaped area, shredding anyone within their range of 100 metres.

The circular compound was now a well-defended combination of base camp and Forward Operating Base.

The camp's construction had taken many days, during which time some of the men, getting their weight, strength and energy back, began to betray their restlessness by playing pranks, first on one another, then on the officers. These began as harmless jokes, usually occurring after an evening of swilling beer, but soon they had become more dangerous.

At first, the most popular pranks were placing a dead snake or jungle rat in someone's basha or sleeping bag, which would only be found when the victim slipped under the sheets or into the bag; putting a decapitated snake's head, amputated rat limb, a few maggots, worms, or dead centipedes or scorpions in someone's bowl of soup, which would only be spotted when the soup was almost finished; or emptying half the water out of someone's full water bottle and filling it up with captured mosquitoes, midges, flies or even wasps, which would frantically burst free when the cap was unscrewed, causing a shock, if not bites or stings, to the victim.

When such pranks became all too easy to anticipate, the more insatiable pranksters, such as Pete Welsh and Alf Laughton moved on to more questionable activities. *Live* snakes, scorpions, centipedes or giant spiders were placed in troopers' kit or weapons, where they could clearly be seen but had to be removed at great personal risk, often when the soldier was in a hurry to report for duty. Minute traces of gunpowder were poked into cigarettes to make them explode when lit, which led to one trooper's face being slightly burned. Seeds that caused unbearable itching were sprinkled inside underclothes and drill fatigues, driving some of the victims frantic when they were on guard or on the firing range. Stinging ants were hidden in soft jungle caps, boots, the pockets of bergens, and even the breeches of weapons, thus causing serious discomfort, often dangerously close to the eyes, sometimes when the victims were in the middle of important activities such as guard duty or jungle patrol.

Great or small, the pranks were not always taken in good spirit and often led to fist fights that had to be broken up by Sergeant Lorrimer. Before long, Lorrimer came to believe that new forms of discipline would have to be imposed and that the men had to be given more to do than simply act as a forward observation unit checking on an enemy that was, to all intents and purposes, invisible.

'Some of the pranks are getting out of hand,' he informed Captain Callaghan, 'and they're the work of men who probably shouldn't have been in this Regiment in the first place — men who transferred for the wrong reasons or were encouraged to do so by NCOs and officers who simply wanted to get shot of them because they were trouble. Unfortunately, we're lumbered with them for now.'

'What men?'

'Troopers Welsh and Laughton, for a start. They play a lot of the pranks, are involved in a lot of fights, and are clearly in the Regiment for the wrong reasons.'

'What reasons?'

'They mistake our lack of authoritarianism, or rather our democratic ways of operating — the Chinese Parliaments and so forth — for a complete lack of discipline. They're cowboys, always looking for some action, and not too fussy about how they get it. They could be trouble, boss. In fact, they already are.'

They were sitting on the verandah under the

overhanging roof of the new HQ building, looking out on the compound where SAS troopers, Gurkhas, Royal Marine Commandos, Sakai labourers, and Iban trackers were either going about their various activities or resting. Some were cleaning weapons, cooking over trench fires, reading maps, writing letters. Others were on guard in the defensive trenches around the camp's perimeter, their Bren guns and M1 carbines aimed at the solid wall of the jungle, just beyond the clear track that ran around the camp and the unseen, deadly Claymore mines placed between the track and the jungle. A football match was in progress in the sports area just west of the HQ. The smoke from the trench fires billowed up and was blown back by the wind, bringing the smell of grilling fish and boiling soup to the nostrils of the hungry Captain Callaghan and Sergeant Lorrimer. The former was smoking a cigarette, sighing as he exhaled.

'It *is* unfortunate,' he said, 'that because of the speed with which the Emergency built up we weren't allowed the luxury of more carefully selecting who we took on. This is now being rectified, but in the meantime, as you rightfully say, we're lumbered with the few remaining undesirables. When this op is over they'll be weeded out and a more stringent selection process applied. For now, I suppose, we'll just have to live with it.'

'I'm worried that the pranks will get worse and the fights more frequent. Either that or one of the pranksters will go too far and do some serious damage.'

'I'm worried about that as well,' Callaghan said.

In fact, they had due cause for concern. As this was a makeshift base camp, there was only one mess, used alike by officers, NCOs and troopers. A couple of days after the completion of the camp, SAS Captain Tony Lidgate was recalled to Johore and due to be lifted out by helicopter the following morning. That evening, he had farewell drinks with Captain Callaghan and other officers and NCOs in the mess, which doubled as a bar and was also filled with hard-drinking troopers. While Lidgate and his friends were standing in a group, drinks in hand, having an animated conversation, not far from a table where Dennis the Menace, Boney Maronie and Dead-Eye were also boozing, a group of SAS troopers, led by Pete Welsh and Alf Laughton, were getting very drunk in their bashas. Knowing what was going on in the mess, they decided to have some sport at the expense of their officers and NCOs.

'Let's scare the shit out of 'em,' Pete Welsh said, 'and set off a little explosion by the mess. They'll jump out of their boots!'

In fact, this had begun when Welsh, a former Sapper with the operational arm of No. 101 Special Training School, Singapore, now the explosive specialist in his four-man team, had been drunkenly boasting about the various ways in which he and other 3rd Corps soldiers had blown up railways and bridges here in Malaya, during the war against the Japanese. When Alf Laughton scoffed at some of the methods described by Welsh, the latter, slurring badly, said he would give them all a demonstration.

While Laughton and the others downed more beer and looked on, Welsh, grinning crazily, removed a small amount of PE (Plastic High-Explosive) from where he had been keeping it, in secret, in his bergen. He also removed a short piece of narrow copper tubing, a phial of acid, a piece of fine wire attached to a simple spring mechanism, a percussion cap and an instantaneous fuse.

'Dead-simple delayed-action device,' he slurred, 'known as a time pencil.'

'Right,' Alf Laughton said, nodding solemnly, 'you mentioned that, mate.'

Welsh nodded as well. They nodded in unison. 'Right,' Welsh slurred, awkwardly making up the simple bomb with blurred vision and shaky hands. 'A time pencil. Dead simple. Put the wire through the tube like this, see? With the spring sticking out one end, right? Then put the phial of acid in the tube as well, see? Like this. Now when I'm ready to set it off, I'll fix the striker to the percussion cap like this. Then I'll squeeze the copper tube to break the phial of acid inside. The acid will eventually eat through this piece of fine wire. When the wire dissolves, the spring will be released and force the striker against the percussion cap – here, see? – which will then ignite the instantaneous fuse and – *voilà*! – up she fucking goes, mate, in fire and smoke. Come on, let's go try it out on those Ruperts over in the mess hut.'

Picking up his home-made bomb and starting out of the basha, Welsh was tugged back by the equally drunken Alf Laughton. 'Hold on,' Laughton said, still holding his bottle of Tiger beer. 'Are we going to have time to get away, Pete?'

'Think I'm fucking dumb? Of *course* we'll've time to get away! The length of delay's reg'lated ... regalate ... 'scuse me, regulated by the thickness of the wire – this, see? – and I've chosen a wire that gives the min'im ... min'mum ... *minimum* period.'

'Whassat, den?' Laughton could hardly speak.

'Thirty minutes.'

'Even *you* can crawl away from the mess in that

time,' Trooper Jack Clayton told him, then broke down in giggles.

'Come on, you dumb cunts, let's go,' Welsh said, staggering out of the basha, carrying his DIY bomb. When the others followed him out, they crossed the dark compound, under the stars that could be seen above the clearing, and made their way, crouched low, often drunkenly falling over, to the 6-foot legs of the raised mess hut.

Huddling under the hut, they tried to stifle their giggling.

'Here,' someone whispered, 'give me a slug from that bottle.'

'Right, mate. That's what friends are for.'

The lights of the hut were filtering out from between the closed shutters, illuminating the hundreds of insects caught and dying in the wire-mesh coverings. They could hear Elvis Presley singing – obviously a radio playing – and loud conversation and laughter from the men.

'Having a fucking good time up there,' Laughton whispered.

'They'll warm up even more,' Welsh replied, 'when this little darlin' goes off. Here, hold my bottle.'

While Laughton held his bottle of Tiger beer, Welsh, still grinning, tied the bomb to one of the legs of the hut, wrapping the string around two or three times, then tugging the knot tight. After checking that the charge was firmly attached, he smirked even more insanely, and said to Laughton: 'Do you want the honour, mate?'

'Yeah,' Laughton slurred. 'Terrific. What I . . .?' He shook his head a few times, blinked rapidly, then cleared his throat and concentrated on his speech. 'What I do, mate?'

Welsh took hold of his right hand and placed it against the narrow copper tube. 'Just squeeze it like you're squeezing a nice piece of tit,' he said. 'Let go when you hear the phial of acid breaking. That's all there is to it.'

'Like this?'

'S'right,' Welsh informed him, still slurring.

Laughton squeezed the phial of acid until he heard it breaking. The sound gave him a bit of a shock and made him jerk his hand away, half expecting the bomb to go off immediately. When it didn't, the other men giggled uncontrollably and Laughton looked at Welsh. 'That it?'

Welsh nodded, grinning like a lunatic. ''At's it, mate,' he slurred. 'Now we better get the fuck out of it.'

They were only halfway back across the compound when the bomb exploded with a roar, blowing the leg to pieces, causing the whole mess hut to keel over like a sinking ship, and instantly setting fire to the timber wall and thatched roof.

The men inside were bawling, rolling across the tilting floor, bouncing off one another or into the tables and chairs that had toppled over and were also on the move. As the flames licked higher and the hut tilted more steeply, some of the men inside burst through the front door or clambered out through windows to drop to the ground, thinking they were being attacked by the CT.

Thinking the same, the men in the defensive trenches opened fire on the dark jungle with their Bren guns and M1 rifles.

The warning siren went off, adding to the general bedlam.

Having thrown themselves to the earth when hearing the explosion, Welsh, Laughton and the other men turned around and sat up, staring in amazement as yellow flames flickered along the wall of the mess hut, then engulfed the thatched roof.

'Shit!' Welsh hissed.

'Jesus Christ!' Laughton whispered.

'We're in for it now,' Jack Clayton said. 'That fucking bomb *worked*, mate!'

When Welsh saw Sergeant Lorrimer walking grimly towards him, he offered his crazy grin.

The next morning, when a surprisingly urbane, even amused, Captain Lidgate had been lifted off by an Army Air Corps Weston Dragonfly helicopter, Callaghan, having assumed command, took the unusual step of holding a disciplinary hearing and fining all of the men known to be involved in the explosion.

While it seemed lenient, the system of fines was one of the punishments Callaghan had decided would be more apt in this particular environment, where being 'confined to barracks' had no relevance whatsoever and imprisonment was out of the question.

Though he intended getting rid of the ringleaders, Welsh and Laughton, when the Regiment returned to Johore, Callaghan withheld this information on the grounds that it would adversely effect their performance while in the *ulu*. Nevertheless, he was now aware that something *had* to be done – as Sergeant Lorrimer had told him more than once.

'There's a lot of energy out there,' Sergeant Lorrimer said after the bombing, 'bottled up and about to explode. That's what caused that unholy prank last night.'

'Then let's give them something to do,' Callaghan replied. 'Let's start the deep reconnaissance patrols. That should burn up their energy.'

'And hopefully kill the bastards,' Lorrimer said. 'That might be a blessing.'

'God's will be done.'

8

The policy of cutting off food and ensuring political isolation had been successful in driving the CT deeper into the jungle. The Security Forces were therefore obliged to pursue the enemy there, which gave the SAS a second chance to prove its value and, at the same time, enabled Captain Callaghan to find work for his more troublesome men.

While relatively orthodox units, such as the Gurkha, Malay, African and Fijian battalions, concentrated on harrying the guerrillas of Johore, Callaghan's men were making their first serious contact with the aboriginal tribes of the interior. Their main task was to protect the Sakai jungle-dwellers, who, being completely at the mercy of the guerrillas, had been forced deeper into their service as a source of food and reluctant manpower. Now Callaghan's men, moving out from the base camp, or Forward Observation Base – for it was, indeed, a combination of both – began to win over these nomad tribesmen, often staying with them for considerable periods of time, sometimes as long as thirteen weeks, before being relieved by other men from the base camp.

One of their main tasks was to build landing strips or helicopter landing pads to enable the aboriginals to sell their supplies. They also brought them medical and engineering aid. In particularly dangerous situations, where the CT were terrorizing a village, the SAS simply moved the whole village and helped the natives rebuild a new home elsewhere. These 'new' communities became known, simply and logically, as 'New Villages'.

Generally speaking, the New Villages needed a remote part of the jungle, well away from any paths which might be used by prying Malays, yet not too far from the kampongs which would supply them with food. A good defensive position was needed for the guard post, if possible on the only way into the camp. Water, and *atap* for thatching, had to be near at hand.

Most of these New Villages, in effect kampongs, all took similar form: a small piece of ground capable of being levelled for a parade ground and a sports ground: two long huts near by for the men: a smaller headquarters housed a little back from the others, a cookhouse, preferably beside a stream, and communal latrines. The villages were then turned into fortresses, in which police posts and even artillery were established.

Much of the success of these New Villages depended on the few lone SAS troopers who lived in them for long periods to sell the aboriginals the idea of self-defence. This was part of the battle for hearts and minds.

For a couple of months Callaghan engaged his SF in Operation Spiderweb, designed to saturate a known CT area with troops so that the guerrillas' mode of life would be disrupted. A concentrated programme of police checks on roads and New Villages was put into action, forcing the bandits to retreat and use up their invaluable food reserves, which were always hidden deep in the *ulu*. When this campaign was in progress, more military units moved in to specific areas where it was hoped, by intensive ambushes and patrols, to force the terrorists out into the open or into the many 'stop' or ambush points established on tracks in the *ulu*.

Helping the SAS were Gurkhas, Royal Marine Commandos, twenty-two Jungle Companies of the Malayan Field Police Force, and Iban trackers from Sarawak, former headhunters who, though fierce fighters, had to be trained by the SAS in the fundamentals of modern soldiering. Now formally

recognized as a locally raised unit of the British
Army and named the Sarawak Rangers, they were
issued with rifles which they used with more enthusiasm than skill. Nevertheless, they were invaluable
as trackers and guides.

Thus, because of Operation Spiderweb, the SAS
was living more and more in the jungle, engaging
in a series of long, arduous, and usually dangerous
operations that certainly burned off the excess
energy of the SAS troublemakers.

A typical CT 'cleansing' operation was a joint
effort between the RAF and the SF. When the
enemy was identified as being concentrated in a
particular area, the RAF would mount a heavy
bombing raid of the jungle location by RAF
Lincolns. A couple of SAS squadrons would
then parachute into the area cleared – or more
accurately, devastated – by the bombing. They
would then either take out the surviving CT
or, if the survivors had fled, take command
of the area, ensuring that any remaining crops
were destroyed, to further deprive the CT of
food.

'The system obviously works,' Captain Callaghan
said to Sergeant Lorrimer during a meeting in the
wood-and-thatch HQ in the jungle base camp, 'but
I view it as an indiscriminate use of air power, as
likely to kill aboriginals as guerrillas. It is, therefore,

in the long run, counterproductive, so I think we should find a better way.'

'I agree. Those bombing raids cause shocking destruction and do often kill the very people we're trying to protect.'

'Any ideas?'

'My belief is that instead of depending on the RAF to clear the way for us, we should concentrate even more on putting small groups of men into the *ulu*. We leave them there for as long as they're required to relay back all the intelligence they can gather on the guerrillas, when not actually harassing them with various acts of sabotage or raids on their camps. They can wage a hearts-and-minds campaign at the same time, thus doubling their effectiveness.'

'I agree with you in principle, but I'm not at all sure how long a small team left to their own devices would remain effective in the *ulu*. They might even go mad.'

'You did it alone for three months. Major Pryce-Jones did it for six. If you can do it, a team of four or five men, even only two, should find it less difficult.'

Callaghan laughed. 'I thought you were going to say easier.'

Lorrimer shook his head, grinning. 'I wouldn't dare.'

'I sometimes think I *did* go mad in that bloody jungle.'

'Not that you'd notice, boss.'

Callaghan grinned and nodded, as if agreeing with Lorrimer's judgement, then became more thoughtful again. 'Well, maybe it's actually easier to do it alone. At least you can only fight with yourself. On the other hand, four or five men, even two, locked together in that isolation, might more quickly get on one another's nerves.'

'I think if we select the right kind of men, we'd be OK. Types like young Parker.'

'Dead-eye Dick.'

'Yes. He hasn't seen action before, but he's a natural if ever I saw one. His endurance during his jungle training was phenomenal. His skill with shotguns and rifles is already the talk of the Regiment, and he can use that crossbow like nobody's business. He also appears to have nerves of steel. What's more, he's modest to the point of shyness.'

'A shy killer,' Callaghan suggested.

'He could be,' Lorrimer replied. 'I've known his type before. There were quite a few in the Long Range Desert Group and we had at least one in Force 136. Modest men, decent in every other respect, but able to kill without qualms. The two combined – the modesty and the killer instinct – make them invaluable.'

'What are you driving at, Sarge?' Callaghan was grinning. 'What are you after?'

'I'm suggesting you let me take a two-man team into the *ulu* and see just how far I can push it, how much we can do.'

'Anything else?'

'Well, I *have* been thinking of our conversation about the lack of time we had to properly pick the kind of men we need for the Regiment. Obviously, we can fix that by weeding out the last of the bad apples, but I still believe that by the time we return to England, we should have evolved a specific, very rigorous selection and training programme that'll ensure only the best make it through. Selection, training, then further training in highly specialized areas. So part of the reason for this jungle hike is to find out just what kind of training will be involved.'

'Right, Sergeant, I'll buy that. Who do you want?'

'Just two men and a Sakai guide, who we'll pick up *en route*. But initially, just two men. Me and . . .'

'Dead-eye Dick.' Callaghan's soft chuckle cut him short. 'Oh, you *are* subtle, Sergeant!'

Now Lorrimer chuckled. 'Well, a man has his reasons.'

'No one else?'

'No. Let's begin modestly to minimize possible damage. Dead-eye's perfect for this.'

'OK, you've got him. When do you want to leave?'

'Tomorrow,' Lorrimer said.

'Aren't you the keen one?' Callaghan sighed, perhaps wishing he could go as well. 'So how do you plan to insert?'

'By parachute.'

'Tree-jumping.'

'Yes.'

'I think we should stop that.'

'There's no other way.'

Callaghan sighed again, this time sadly. 'No, I suppose not.'

By now the SAS had made frequent parachute jumps into the *ulu* and suffered many casualties in their dangerous attempts to perfect tree-jumping. These casualties had occurred mainly because of the unpredictable behaviour of the parachutes as they were 'bounced' by the thermal effect of air above the trees. However, in the view of many officers, including Callaghan, the technique of abseiling out of the trees was also proving to be more dangerous than it was worth.

In theory, the soldier detached himself from his parachute, lashed a long webbing strap to a branch, and descended safely to the ground.

In practice, however, the webbing often bulged at intervals, where it had been stitched, and therefore snagged at high speed as it travelled through the D-rings on the soldier's harnesses. All too frequently this would jerk him to a violent halt, sometimes smashing him against the tree, resulting in broken bones or even death, the latter usually occurring when the parachutist, badly hurt and unable to stand the pain, cut himself loose from his snagged harness and fell at least 100 feet to the forest floor. Nevertheless, as tree-jumping was the only way to get into the areas cleared by the RAF bombing raids, it remained the Standard Operating Procedure of the campaign.

'Well,' Lorrimer said after a long silence, 'do I have your permission?'

'If you're going to do it, I suppose you're going to do it. The quicker the better, Sarge. Tomorrow it is.'

'Thanks, boss,' Lorrimer said, beaming with pleasure. 'I'd better get started straight away then; fix things up with Dead-eye.'

'Yes, Sergeant, you do that.'

Lorrimer left the HQ, almost dancing down the steps of the verandah under the overhanging roof of thatched palms, then walked the short distance to the radio shack. Once there, he had the on-duty trooper, Trooper Jack Clayton, radio back to Johore to say that he would require a Beverley for a two-man parachute jump, taking off approximately at first light. Leaving the radio shack, he went to the nearby helicopter landing pad where the pilot, Lieutenant Ralph Ellis of the Army Air Corps, was, as usual, lovingly tending his Sikorski S-55 Whirlwind.

'Pissing around as usual, are you, boss?' Sergeant Lorrimer said in the informal manner already ingrained in the SAS.

Lieutenant Ellis grinned. 'Keeps me busy, Sarge. What can I do for you?'

'I need to be flown back to Johore with another man tomorrow morning, a couple of hours before first light.

Ellis winced. 'You mean I have to get out of bed?'

''Fraid so, boss.'

'Four a.m.?'

'That sounds reasonable.'

'Who's the other man?'

'Trooper Richard Parker.'

'Dead-eye.'

'Correct.'

'What are you two up to, Sarge?'

'We're making a jump into the *ulu* and the Beverleys can't land here.'

'That's why I love my helicopter,' Ellis said,

stroking the green-painted fuselage of his beloved Whirlwind. 'She can go fast or slow, move up or down, take any number of positions. She's a real little beauty.'

Lorrimer grinned at the sexual connotations. 'No wonder you guys are glamorous to the ladies. I'm in the wrong business.'

'I would have to agree, Sarge.'

'Four a.m.?'

'I'll be here,' Ellis said.

'Good. See you then, boss.' Lorrimer turned away and crossed the sports ground to the spider, which, like the other buildings, was raised off the ground and made from timber and palm leaves and thatched with *atap*. On the sports ground near the barracks a few of the troopers, stripped to the waist and gleaming with sweat, were kicking a football between them in a desultory manner. Some of their mates were sitting around slugging Tiger beer from bottles and either idly watching their friends playing or enjoying the sunset. Gurkhas were relaxing on the verandah of their own barracks, as were the few remaining Royal Marine Commandos. The small group of Sarawak Rangers had their own quarters: a thatched house of the kind they would have lived in in Borneo and which they had constructed themselves. Trench fires were smoking around the sports ground and the inviting smell of cooking food filled the cooling evening air, doubtless tormenting the men in the defensive trenches located around the circular compound and facing out towards the jungle.

Entering the gloomy spider, which now had fans in the ceiling and was therefore much cooler than outside, Lorrimer marched between the facing rows of timber-and-thatch bashas, nodding at some of the men as he passed. Pete Welsh was lying flat on his back, stark naked, with an impressive erection, listening to Elvis Presley singing about teddy bears on the radio. On the bed beside him, Alf Laughton, completely ignoring Welsh's erection, was biting his lower lip as he concentrated on writing a letter home. Other men were also listening to radios, writing letters, leafing through pin-up magazines or books, smoking or checking their personal kit.

Lorrimer stopped when he came to young Dead-eye, who was sitting on the edge of his bed, meticulously cleaning his standard-issue M1 carbine. His 9mm Browning High Power handgun was lying on the bed, polished and oiled. Also on the bed, all polished, were his bayonet, Fairburn-Sykes commando knife and *parang*. Dead-eye, it was clear, took good care of his personal equipment.

'Hi, boss,' he said, looking up at Lorrimer with his steady, oddly opaque grey gaze and hesitant smile. 'You want me?'

'I'm thinking of going for a little hike into the jungle. Long-term. Just you and me. Doing anything and everything. It's kind of an experiment, so you don't have to come if you don't want to. You have to volunteer, kid.'

'I volunteer,' Dead-eye said.

'We leave for Johore by chopper at four in the morning, then fly in by Beverley from there.'

'Tree-jumping?'

'Yes.'

'What do I need?'

'What you've got here, plus a full kit, smoke, phosphorus and fragmentation grenades, flares, PRC 319, SARBE beacon, a 9mm Owen submachine-gun, a Browning 12-gauge autoloader shotgun and the crossbow.'

'Sounds like fun,' Dead-eye said.

'It just might be. Do you have any questions?'

'No,' Dead-eye said. 'Four a.m. at the chopper pad, then.'

'That's it. But make sure you collect those other weapons tonight.'

'Will do, Sarge.'

Lorrimer was walking back out of the barracks

when Dennis the Menace and Boney Maronie entered, both stripped to the waist and covered in sweat. Lorrimer stopped to ask: 'What have you two been up to? You look all hot and bothered. Having a little hanky-panky, were you?'

'Hey, give us a break, Sarge!' Boney Maronie said, outraged. 'I'm as straight as they come.'

'Not as straight as that erection on Pete Welsh,' Lorrimer said. 'He must have it up for sale.'

Both men glanced along the spider at Pete Welsh's impressive erection, which Welsh himself was ignoring.

'Mmmmm,' Boney Maronie said. 'About half the size of mine. He wants someone to give it a tug and make it grow bigger.'

'Why don't you help him out instead of making each other sweat in mysterious ways?'

'Football,' Dennis the Menace said firmly. 'No more and no less, Sarge. We were both playing football. So what are you doing here?'

'I came to invite Dead-eye for an extended trip into the jungle.'

'Extended? How long?'

'Two or three weeks. Maybe longer.'

'Just you and Dead-eye?' Boney Maronie asked.

'That's right.'

'Sounds real cosy,' Dennis the Menace said with

a wicked grin. 'Going to work up a sweat between you, are you?'

'*Touché*,' Lorrimer said, grinning and waving his right hand as he left the spider.

9

Looking down through one of the many windows of the almost empty Beverley, Dead-eye could see the canopy of the jungle, stretching out to the horizon like a green sea gaining colour in the brightening pearly-grey light of dawn. The trees looked impenetrable, like an almost solid mass. It was hard to believe that beneath them were streams, waterfalls, swamps, a myriad of wildlife, thriving Sakai kampongs – and approximately 2,000 Communist guerrillas. It was also hard to believe that you could actually parachute down and find enough space between the trees to reach the ground. Nevertheless, that was what he would be doing in a few minutes' time.

'We're coming in low,' the RAF Loadmaster said. 'Three hundred and fifty metres, to be precise. So you better be quick, boys.'

'No sweat,' Sergeant Lorrimer said. 'We've often

come in even lower than that, so we're not so concerned.'

'The brave lads of the SAS,' said the Loadmaster in an ironic voice. 'I'd like to recommend my mother-in-law to the Regiment. I desperately need to get rid of her.'

It was a backhanded compliment that made Lorrimer grin, while also reminding him and Dead-eye that the jump they were about to make was not without danger.

'You OK?' Lorrimer asked.

'Sure,' Dead-eye replied, meaning it, secretly thrilled that Lorrimer had chosen him above all the others for this special task.

Inevitably, the rest of the lads had given him a terrible ribbing the night before, making the anticipated jokes about 'hot-bedding' with Sergeant Lorrimer and how older men lusted after white-cheeked cherry boys. It was all good-natured fun and Dead-eye didn't mind it a bit, though he wished they'd stop calling him a 'cherry boy', which was a George Town whore's term for a male virgin. He didn't have a steady girlfriend, but Dead-eye was no virgin.

In fact, he'd lost his virginity at sixteen to an older woman, a so-called 'aunt', actually a girlfriend of his father's. Since then he'd had it pretty regularly, occasionally with girls his own age, but mostly with rather older women, whom he found were content with the sex and didn't expect too many sweet words from him.

Dead-eye was uncomfortable with conversation in general, but even more so with the endearments that most girls of his own age expected. Having spent his formative years watching his father beat his mother, he didn't have much faith in romantic love.

His father was a long-distance lorry driver, born and bred in West Croydon, which he had never left, except when driving across Britain or on the Continent. Parker senior was an alcoholic who liked football, darts, horse-racing, the dogs and women, in that order; but his wife came last on his long list of the latter.

Dead-eye had spent most of his childhood huddling in corners in his parents' house on a West Croydon council estate, looking on in terror and incomprehension as his father, roaring drunk, took out his spleen with fist and boot on his wife. Eventually, when Dead-eye was twelve or thirteen, he attempted to defend his mother and was pummelled almost senseless for his troubles.

Thereafter, like a wild animal smelling blood, Dead-eye's father started beating him instead of his mother. The teenager took this as a kind of victory, but when he received no thanks from his mother – who by now was deadening her pain by joining her husband in his drinking binges – he retreated into himself and gazed out upon the world with gravely suspicious eyes.

By the time he was eighteen, Dead-eye had realized that the only way he could retain his dignity was to leave home for good. Wanting to travel but not having the money to do so, needing adventure but not knowing how to find it, he took the only option that someone with his education, or lack of it, could take: he enlisted in the Army.

It was the best thing he could possibly have done. After passing his three months of basic training with flying colours, he was posted to the 2nd Battalion, Royal Regiment of Fusiliers, where his prowess on the firing range soon became almost legendary. Gratified by this, gaining pride and dignity from it, he realized that while he loved being a soldier, he still needed to do more than he was doing, which was basically an uninspiring routine of drill, training, and guard duties. So, when he heard that the renowned World War Two regiment, the SAS was being reformed to fight the war, or the Emergency, in Malaya, he applied to join. Though the selection process was brutally hard, he again passed with flying colours and soon found himself on a Hercules C-130, bound for Malaya. He had never been happier.

Now, sitting beside Sergeant Lorrimer in the otherwise empty hold of the Beverley, he felt that he was in very good company.

He was well aware of the fact that Lorrimer, apart from being a naturally likeable man, was a veteran of World War Two, a former member of the legendary Long Range Desert Group, then of the original 1 SAS, also in North Africa, and finally of Force 136, the clandestine resistance unit set up by the Special Operations Executive during World War Two for operations in Japanese-occupied Malaya.

In fact, Lorrimer was the kind of soldier that Dead-eye eventually wanted to become. Admiring and respecting the older man, he was truly proud to have been picked to be his partner for this dangerous mission.

'Stand up!' the Loadmaster bawled, opening the starboard door in the fuselage and letting the slipstream roar in. 'Action stations!'

'Hi, ho,' Sergeant Lorrimer said. 'On your feet, kid.'

'Aye, aye, boss.'

Dead-eye and Lorrimer stood up together, both heavily burdened with their parachutes, packed bergens, bandoliers, webbing and weapons.

'I'll go out first as the drifter,' Sergeant Lorrimer said to Dead-eye as the Loadmaster, whipped by the roaring slipstream, placed the boxed supplies by the open door, preparing to parachute them down into the jungle. 'Stay close behind me and as soon as I go out, place yourself on the ramp and wait until you see my parachute open. Only jump when you've checked the strength and direction of the wind from my decent.'

'Right, boss, I've got it.'

'I'm not finished yet.' Sergeant Lorrimer was being serious. 'When you're descending and have popped your parachute, keep your eyes on the jungle canopy, as well as on me, to ensure that you not only fall close to me, but drop down through a clearing in the forest. The supplies will go down first and we'll pick them up when we land. Have you got that?'

'Yes, Sarge.'

Lorrimer patted Dead-eye on the shoulder. 'I'm sure you have,' he said, then turned away to take his position behind the boxed supplies piled up near the open door.

The Loadmaster raised the thumb of his right hand, then pushed the wooden crates out. Being on static lines, the parachutes on the crates would be deployed at a predetermined height by a line connected to the aircraft. When the Loadmaster had checked that the chutes had opened success- fully, he disconnected the static lines and waved

Lorrimer forward. Using standard-issue Irvin-X Type parachutes, Lorrimer and Dead-eye would have to 'pop' them themselves.

Lorrimer braced himself on the rim of the doorway, his body being whipped by the roaring slipstream. When the Loadmaster patted him on the shoulder and bawled 'Right!', Lorrimer threw himself out.

As soon as Lorrimer had disappeared, Dead-eye took his place on the edge of the doorway, holding on to the sides to keep the roaring wind from sucking him out. Looking down, he saw Lorrimer being swept briefly, violently sideways on the slipstream, above the already opened parachutes of the supply crates; then, escaping from it, dropping like a stone towards the jungle canopy 1,000 feet below. Almost immediately – or, to be more precise, as soon as he fell vertically – Lorrimer released his parachute. Dead-eye saw it billowing up like a white flower in that sea of sun-streaked greenery. Both the Loadmaster and Dead-eye watched Lorrimer's descent, gauging from it the strength and direction of the wind; then, as if thinking in tandem, the Loadmaster patted Dead-eye's shoulder, bawled 'Right', and Dead-eye threw himself out.

There was an even louder roaring. The breath was dragged from his lungs. The next thing he knew – though by now he was getting used to it – he was free of the slipstream, releasing his parachute, and floating down through the air, dazzled by the vast blue sweep of the morning sky, then by the approaching sea of green jungle, feeling magically, even transcendentally, alive.

Immediately below him, he saw the billowing white flower of Sergeant Lorrimer's parachute. Below that, he saw the smaller chutes of the supply crates – at least they looked smaller because they were further down – already nearing the dense jungle canopy.

As the first of the supply crates made contact with the canopy, either becoming tagged on the treetops or smashing on down to the jungle floor, Dead-eye used the strings on his chute to manoeuvre in the direction of Lorrimer. The descent was very quick, leaving little time for calculation, and Lorrimer was already disappearing through the treetops when Dead-eye managed to head in his direction. By the time Lorrimer had disappeared, the trees were rushing up at Dead-eye ever faster. He saw a gap and tried to manoeuvre into it, but hit the treetops anyway.

The former silence of his descent exploded with the sounds of his fall, as huge palm leaves, branches, creeping vines and creepers tried to ensnare him, then broke and gave way to let him fall through. He was trapped, stopped, broke free, fell again, then heard a snapping, cracking and hissing as he bounced, twisted and fell through showering leaves, flowers, broken branches and tendrils of rattan. He stopped about 30 feet above the ground, span rapidly, smashed into sharp branches and thorns, then came to a standstill, dangling in mid-air on the end of his harness.

Dazed, he blinked repeatedly, breathed deeply, then looked down at the jungle floor.

Lorrimer, already divested of his parachute and bergen, was looking up at him from a dark hole that Dead-eye soon realized was just the ground way below.

'Are you all right?' Lorrimer bawled.

'Yes!' Dead-eye bawled back.

'You'll have to abseil the rest of the way. Come on, kid, get moving!'

Feeling that he was being dragged down by the weight of his combined parachute, packed bergen, webbing, bandoliers and strapped-on weapons, Dead-eye was convinced he was about to fall. In the event, he didn't. Extremely calmly and carefully, he uncoiled his knotted rope, tied it around a particularly thick branch, let the rest of it drop down to the jungle floor, then used his commando knife to cut his parachute harness away from the foliage and started lowering himself down on the rope, using the knots as convenient grips. The combined weight of his bergen and other kit caused him agony, but eventually, when only 10 feet above the ground, he was able to let the rope go and drop the rest of the way. He fell in a clattering tangle of kit and weapons, feeling battered and bruised, into a thick carpet of dead leaves and seedling trees.

Picking himself up, he saw Lorrimer grinning at him.

'About bloody time,' the Sergeant said. 'The supplies all dropped in the vicinity, so let's go and collect them.'

'Yes, boss,' Dead-eye said.

10

Lone men in the jungle require the skills of the hunter: concealment, tracking, endurance, coolness and a lethally accurate shot. All of these were abilities perfected by Sergeant Lorrimer during his time with Force 136 in Malaya in 1943. Combined with them were a quick intelligence, relentless determination, and a good ear for foreign languages. As the admiring Dead-eye soon found out, the Yorkshireman could fire his Browning 12-gauge autoloader shotgun with high accuracy at a speed which made the first half-dozen shots seem like one. He could also speak fluent Malay, Chinese and Siamese, which gave him another advantage in the *ulu*.

Indeed, their first stop after the first day's gruelling hike through the gloomy, humid jungle, heavily burdened with their overpacked bergens, weapons and supplies, was a Sakai house which, like all such houses, was built on a slope to ensure that the front was high above the ground. It consisted of one large room, about 30 feet square, under a single ridge of *atap* thatching, with each gable extended to form lengthy extensions to the main room. Except for the uprights of the house, the whole framework was of bamboo. The floor was of symmetrical slats of bamboo lashed with fine rattan to the floor joists with a 'breathing' space between each slat. The main part of the house was surrounded by a balustrade of flattened bamboo surmounted by a single large bamboo, which fenced off the extensions so that they resembled loose boxes. They were used as guest rooms. The ridge of *atap* thatch that extended over the railing at night was rolled back during the day to let in cool air and light.

The house belonged to the village head, Abang Kasut, an old friend of Lorrimer's from the days when they had fought the Japanese together. Abang was a well-fed, amiable man who looked slightly licentious and self-satisfied. This could have been because he had a very large family, including many wives, all of whom were bare-breasted, wearing only a *sarong* of cloth or bark. Some had red, white or ochre paint smeared on their faces, and a few were ornamented with a matchstick thrust through the piece of flesh below and between the nostrils. All were smoke-stained and unwashed, but a few were beautiful, with luxuriant black hair tied in a bun held up with a bamboo comb. Their children, with round, dark eyes and pot bellies, seemed very happy.

'You live in the wrong country, my young friend,' Abang informed Dead-eye, noting how he could hardly take his eyes off the bare-breasted women. 'A man requires so many different things in a woman, he is hardly likely to find it in one, so he needs many wives. This is more civilized, yes?'

'I'm not sure that the wives would agree,' Dead-eye replied.

'Of course they do,' Abang insisted. 'Having to share my attentions with all the others removes the great burden of a single wife's servitude. They are happier this way.'

'And I'm sure *you're* not suffering, Abang,' Sergeant Lorrimer said.

The aboriginal roared with laughter, slapped his own pot belly, then poured liquid from a jar into three glasses. 'Here,' he said, handing a glass each to Lorrimer and Dead-eye, 'have a drink of *samsu*. It will make you feel less tired.'

In certain ways, being in this village was like returning to the Stone Age. The youths and older men carried 8-foot blow-pipes with bamboo quivers for poisoned arrows ornamented with strange conventional designs. Dressed only in a scanty loincloth, each carried on his back a small bag closely woven with fine rattan to hold his tobacco, flint, steel and tinder. The older men also carried an apparatus for preparing betel nut for chewing. Many of them wore strings of coloured beads looped over their shoulders, crossing front and behind, with more beads or an amulet of some kind around their necks. Some also wore a circle of woven and patterned bark to keep their hair in place, invariably with bright flowers tucked into it.

Lorrimer and Dead-eye spent the night in the headman's house, enjoying a lengthy meal of turtle soup followed by a combination of pig, *kijang* (barking deer), monkey and snake meat, with side dishes of sweet potatoes, lizard eggs, mixed vegetables with spices and ginger, and fried rice. This gourmet banquet was washed down with more *samsu*, a strong spirit distilled from rice, which soon got them drunk, encouraging Lorrimer and Abang to reminisce fondly about old times.

It did not escape Dead-eye's attention that when they discussed the fate of old friends from the war, both British and Sakai, a surprising number of them – indeed, the majority – had been captured and beheaded by the Japanese.

Nevertheless, clearly inspired by such recollections to have another adventure, Abang agreed to

join them the next morning as their guide through
the jungle.

'It will make me feel young again,' he said. 'I
grow fat and lazy in this village, being served hand
and foot. You come here to save me from myself,
so how can I say no?'

Though stowing a lot of their gear in a covered
trench beneath Abang's raised house, where it
would not be found if the CT turned up, they
moved out at first light still carrying 25-pound
loads each, including a 9mm Owen sub-machine-
gun, one Browning 12-gauge autoloader shotgun,
full magazines for both weapons, the crossbow
with 24 lightweight slim alloy bolts and arrows,
six No. 80 white phosphorus incendiary hand-
grenades, 9mm Browning High Power handguns,
a week's food, water bottles, one change of
clothes, groundsheets without blankets, a pair
of field-glasses, a button compass and small-scale
maps, *parangs*, commando knives, fishing line and
hooks, and a basic medical kit that included
antibiotics, antihistamine, water-sterilizing tablets,
anti-malaria tablets, painkillers, and a good supply
of waterproof plasters and bandages.

'No condoms,' Sergeant Lorrimer joked to Dead-
eye. 'That means you're in for some real work.'

It did not take long for Dead-eye to understand
why they needed an aboriginal guide, no matter

how well they had been trained at Johore. Born and bred in the *ulu*, Abang had a keen eye for the most minute traces of human movement through the jungle, such as dislodged pieces of bark, broken branches, twisted leaves, threads of clothing caught on twigs, and even broken spiders' webs. Sometimes the terrorists would deliberately go without shoes in the hopes of making the Security Forces think the footprints were those of aboriginals, but Abang could tell the difference because, as he informed Lorrimer and Dead-eye, the aboriginals had splayed toe-prints whereas the terrorist footprint revealed toes cramped in by being normally encased in shoes or boots. Abang even showed them where some terrorists had attempted to blur their tracks by treading lightly in the footmarks of an elephant.

'They often use the footmarks of a *seladang* as well,' he said. 'The wild ox or bison of Malaya. Unless you look with extreme care, you will see only the footmark of the animal, not of the man.'

'This information is invaluable,' Sergeant Lorrimer told him. 'However, our first requirement is for a long-term hide-out from which we can forage through the *ulu* at will.'

'I have just the place,' Abang replied with confidence.

He led them upstream, across a high pile of fallen

trees, along a side stream, and through a bamboo thicket which retained no footprints. Following a narrow track slightly uphill, they came to a trench about 6 feet deep, 3 feet wide and 30 feet long, opening at its far end into a chamber about 12 feet square and 10 feet high, hollowed out of a steep bank of red clay and scrub-covered rock. This natural cave was covered by a belt of tangled bamboo 40 feet high, which would hide the smoke of a camp-fire. Surprisingly, the hollow was filled with old packing crates.

'I lived here for months,' Abang explained, 'to avoid the Japanese during the war. Later, I used it to hide from Ah Hoi's guerrillas. I am still alive, so it must be a safe place.'

Using a *changkol* – the large hoe which replaces the spade in Malaya – each of the men dug himself a scrape to lie in. A large tent was raised over the three scrapes. The *changkol* was also used to level a platform outside the tent, where they placed a crude table and chairs made from the packing crates. Over this they placed bamboo split in half and laid alternate ways up to make a covering against the rain. In a small patch of garden, they found plenty of edible tapioca.

Lorrimer and Dead-eye then settled in to learn about survival in this alien environment. They were taught well by Abang.

For the first few meals they caught fish by dropping small charges of gelignite into the pools. The tiny explosions dazed the fish, which could then be lifted out by hand – a process that required no great skill and was known to most of the SAS troopers. Later, however, when Abang took them over, they explored the jungle in search of pig, *kijang* and even monkeys. The pigs were scarce, but they managed to shoot a few barking deer.

To attract the deer, Abang would hide in the jungle and give out a piercing scream with the aid of a small section of bamboo split in a traditional Sakai manner. If there were any *kijang* within earshot, they would reply with their harsh bark and come closer, doing so each time Abang gave out his scream, until finally they were in range of Lorrimer's shotgun.

Dead-eye began using his standard-issue M1 carbine for anything larger than monkeys, though in the jungle, as he soon noticed, you rarely get a good shot at anything over fifty yards away. Nevertheless, he soon became as good as Lorrimer, and between them, with Abang's expert guidance, they shot, cooked and ate a wide variety of animals, including pigs, deer and monkeys, although the latter were low on their list of truly tasty food.

In the swamps there were a great many mud turtles, which are about the size of half a football.

Abang taught Lorrimer and Dead-eye to look for a slight cloudiness in the mud, which was an indication of the movement of a turtle just below the surface. When they saw the movement, they simply scooped the turtle up with their hands. The resulting soup was delicious – it included lichens and mosses soaked overnight in clean water – and the meat, when served on its own, was very tender and tasty.

Though less fun to catch or cook, snakes also made excellent food, being similar in taste and texture to a mixture of chicken and lobster. After Abang had removed the poisonous secretions on the skin or the venom glands from the head (in the latter case he removed the entire head) the snakes were gutted, then cooked in their skins by being placed on hot embers and turned constantly. When the heat caused the skin to split, the meat was removed and boiled. Cooked in a similar manner was the monitor lizard – a reptile 6 or 7 feet in length – whose eggs were also delicious and could be used in mixed-vegetable salads. Frogs, which had poisonous skins, were first skinned, then gutted and roasted on sticks.

On the ground of the jungle were snakes, centipedes, scorpions and giant spiders. These were dangerous. Just as dangerous, however, was the *seladang*, the wild ox or bison, which would attack humans on sight. Nevertheless, with Abang's help, they managed to shoot one and found, to their surprise, that the meat went down well with rice, sweet potato and vegetables, preferably followed by sweet coffee, *samsu* and a good cheroot. Finally, on the correct assumption that meat would not always be available, Abang taught them how to pick out edible fungi, leaves, nuts, roots, berries, and fruit from the *ulu*'s wide variety of produce, much of which was poisonous. The more edible fruits and plants had to be brought down from the jungle canopy, which entailed an arduous, dangerous climb and descent, though they soon mastered this without the aid of their abseiling ropes.

'Living off the fat of the land,' Dead-eye said after one particularly enjoyable meal of turtle soup, snake stew, wild figs, mango and coconut juice mixed with *samsu*. 'This is better than life back at home.'

Sergeant Lorrimer did not reply. He was too busy jotting down notes for the report which, as he had explained, would be the basis for a more rigorous SAS Selection, Training and Cross-Training programme, to be introduced when the Regiment was back in England.

'What's Cross-Training?' Dead-eye asked.

'Such innocence!' Sergeant Lorrimer replied. 'You're already doing it, kid.'

Before setting out on patrols in search of the CT, Lorrimer, Dead-eye and Abang practised walking and running past each other to make sure that no bit of metal caught the light and nothing could betray them by its rattle, such as ammunition, metallic kit or half-used boxes of matches. They even wrapped their weapons in adhesive tape to stop them shining in the moonlight.

With a little practice, they learned to walk heel first on hard ground and toe first on softer ground, so that they passed absolutely silently and were, with their camouflaged clothes and darkened faces, virtually invisible.

To walk in this way required much practice. As it called for the use of muscles not normally used, it was initially exhausting, though eventually it became second nature to them.

To follow a jungle path, even on a moonlit night, it was necessary to use light of some sort, so they put a green leaf inside the glass, not only to make the torch less bright, but to accustom their eyes to a dim light. If the battery ran out, a few fireflies or luminous centipedes in the reflector of the torch gave just enough light to read a map, lay a charge or even follow a path through the *ulu*.

GUERRILLAS IN THE JUNGLE

The three of them temporarily gave up smoking because the use of tobacco affects one's sense of smell – and that was often the first means they had of detecting a nearby enemy. Also, they evolved a special system of signals that made talk unnecessary. One was a clicking noise between the upper teeth and side of the tongue – the sound used to encourage a horse. This was an excellent signal, being made very softly yet carrying a great distance on a still night. Even if the enemy heard it, they would probably mistake it for a bird, an insect or a rubber nut falling off a tree. A single click meant 'Stop' or 'Danger'.

The only other signal they needed was a rallying cry. For this they imitated the hunting cry of Britain's tawny owl, a piercing sound which carries a great distance even in thick woodland. It cannot be confused with any other cry heard in the Malayan jungle, yet to the uninitiated it passes without notice in the wide variety of weird nocturnal sounds.

Occasionally they would catch a brief glimpse of a jungle tiger, a few leaf-eating monkeys or some noisy gibbons. There were abundant signs of pig in the deep, muddy puddles which were their wallows, and where the rivers were bordered by meadows of green grass, kept short by water buffalo, or Chinese vegetable gardens.

The leeches, which were everywhere, were tormenting. By now, however, Lorrimer and Dead-eye had become inured to them (Abang hardly noticed them) and followed the Chinese custom of putting a pinch of their reddish fine-cut tobacco on each bite. This congealed the blood and stopped it flowing, but before long their legs, particularly the shins and ankles, were covered in suppurating, stinking sores about an inch across and a quarter of an inch deep. Pus poured out of them and, as a result of infection, the lymphatic glands in their groins became so painful and swollen that at times they could hardly walk, much less go hunting or on recce patrols. When sulphathiazole powder had also failed to cure them, they managed to draw the pus from the wounds by smearing the tar-like Chinese substance, *kow-yok*, on a piece of cloth and covering the wounds with it. This treatment also protected the wounds from the water.

Once on patrol, they were surprised by the number of rivers they had to cross. The jungle sometimes rose to hundreds of feet, from which altitude, through windows in the jungle wall, they could see its sheer extent, as well as the many rubber estates further west. Those steep hills, however, also turned some of the many rivers into foaming torrents that rushed, roaring, between boulders, slabs of granite and high mud banks.

Sometimes they took boats, less than 10 feet long and pointed at each end. With the two bergens in the stern, the three men could fit in, one behind the other, if they stretched out their legs on either side of the man in front. Abang also taught them to build two different kinds of jungle raft.

The bamboo raft consisted of two layers of thick bamboo in lengths of 10 feet. Holes were pierced through the bamboo canes near both ends and in the middle. Thin stakes were passed through the holes to connect the bamboo canes together. The canes were then lashed to the stakes with twine, rattan or strong vines. The second deck of the raft was made exactly the same way and laid on top of the first. The two layers were then lashed together.

The gripper bar raft, which was even quicker to build, required logs for the deck and four thick, slightly pliable stakes, long enough to overlap the width of the deck. Two of the stakes were placed on the ground, spaced apart to make a distance slightly shorter than the length of the logs. The logs were laid over the stakes, overlapping to similar lengths each end. The other stakes were placed on top of the logs, parallel with the stakes on the bottom. Each pair of stakes was tied firmly together on one side. A man standing on the logs then held the stakes down on the other side while a second man lashed them together so that the logs were gripped firmly between them.

Both rafts could be steered with the aid of a simple paddle rudder mounted on an A-frame near one end of the deck. The A-frame was secured to the four corners of the raft with guy ropes and the rudder was tied to the A-frame to prevent it from slipping. The rudder could then also be used as a 'sweep' for propulsion. Though primitive, both rafts were perfectly adequate for travel on all but the most violent of rivers.

Often, after coming in off the cooling river or emerging soaked in sweat from the *ulu*'s dreadful humidity, they would spend the night in a deserted Sakai village, where all the houses were made of bamboo and raised on stilts.

'The villages are deserted,' Abang explained, 'either because the Sakai are up on high ground, clearing the jungle to grow tapioca and maize, or because they're fleeing from Ah Hoi's guerrillas. Ah Hoi is committing dreadful atrocities to terrorize the whole *ulu*.'

Many of the Malay kampongs, also, were deserted and once or twice the three-man team spent the night there. One night was spent in a deserted charcoal-burner's hut, drinking *samsu*; another in a coffee house run by a wizened old

Chinese man whose coffee was strongly alcoholic.
They slept drunkenly and soundly those nights.

For spying purposes, Lorrimer and Dead-eye would
sometimes pass themselves off as Malays or Chinese.
But the easiest way was to disguise themselves as
Indians and dress like Tamils, wearing the standard
white shirt, a *dhoti* or *sarong* around the waist,
and a white cloth, deliberately dirtied, around
the head and hanging down behind. Their com-
plexions were darkened with a mixture of coffee,
lamp-black, iodine and potassium permanganate.
On such missions, they always kept a pistol and a
hand-grenade tucked into the tops of their *sarongs*
in case of emergency.

Often, they saw Malay cyclists or Tamil bullock-
carts moving along the muddy, narrow paths by
the river. Following the tracks of these people
invariably brought them to a Sakai village or
Malay kampong where they would pick up more
info on the movements of Ah Hoi's guerrillas.
Though Ah Hoi's main body of guerrillas seemed
to be truly invisible, the three-man team often
came across isolated bands of roving guerrillas
or, possibly, bandits who had to be 'neutralized',
'taken out' or 'despatched' with ruthless efficiency.
This Lorrimer and Dead-eye did with the Browning Autoloader shotgun, the M1 carbine, No.

80 white-phosphorus incendiary hand-grenades, home-made bombs, and even, on occasions when silent killing was necessary, with their Fairburn-Sykes commando knives or the crossbow.

Dead-eye was the one who always used the crossbow and he was deadly with it, usually putting the lightweight slim alloy bolt and arrow into his victim's heart, or through the back or side of his neck, with unerring accuracy.

'You have the eyes of a fucking hawk,' Lorrimer told him, 'and you're just as deadly.'

When engaged in their murderous activities, the team's routine was to leave the hide-out at last light, with their faces and hands darkened, wearing battledress carefully camouflaged with patches of mud. Each of them carried a main weapon, such as the 9mm Owen sub-machine-gun, the M1 carbine or the Browning shotgun. They also carried a 9mm Browning High Power handgun and a couple of No. 80 grenades or home-made bombs. The latter were made by putting a stick of gelignite, with detonator and fuse attached, inside a tin or a section of bamboo, then filling it up with several pounds of road metal. The fuse was lit by pressing a small igniter in a copper tube, obviating the need for matches. One great advantage of making their own was that they could vary the length of the fuses, so that the explosions would continue for some time after they left the scene. This would keep the guerrillas from answering their fire or following them until they were well away from the scene.

Once, encouraged by Abang, they followed the tracks of four men for five days until they spotted the hut occupied by the guerrillas. Settling down a good distance away, they waited for an impending rainstorm to arrive. When, as they had anticipated, the sentries took shelter from the rain, Abang, Lorrimer and Dead-eye crept up to within five yards of the soaked, still smouldering camp-fire. Lorrimer then pressed the igniter on a home-made bomb and lobbed it straight through the open entrance of the thatched hut. The guerrillas screamed in panic just before the bomb exploded, destroying most of the hut and setting what was left of it on fire. When two of the four guerrillas staggered shrieking from the swirling smoke and flames, both of them on fire, they were cut down by Dead-eye, who used his M1 with methodical, fearsome efficiency.

Occasionally the team separated to pursue guer-rillas who had deliberately split up to elude them. Lorrimer would not normally have done this, but he made an exception in Dead-eye's case, confident that the young man was at his best when left to himself.

He was correct in this assumption. Armed with
his M1, which he could now fire as rapidly and
accurately as Lorrimer fired his Browning shotgun,
and employing the aboriginal tracking knowledge
he had gleaned from Abang, Dead-eye pursued his
quarry relentlessly through the jungle, from early
afternoon to last light. Finally realizing that he
could not elude this mad dog of an Englishman,
the guerrilla turned around to face him in a jungle
clearing. The two men were barely 20 yards apart.
Dead-eye fired six rapid repeat shots with his M1,
so fast they were like a single shot, and the guerrilla
was picked up and slammed back down on the
jungle floor, his hand frozen around his unfired
weapon.

Dead-eye didn't even bother to check that the
man was dead; he just turned away and retraced
his own route back through the trees.

'You're pretty good,' Lorrimer said, when Dead-
eye had finished reporting to him in their hide-out.
'You're almost as quick as me now.'

'Quicker,' Dead-eye firmly corrected him, without a trace of irony.

'If you say so, kid.'

The truth of this assertion became plain when,
on the next patrol, Lorrimer insisted that Dead-eye
act as back-marker to him and Abang, who was
at the front as tracker. When they encountered a

guerrilla, who burst out of the jungle firing from the hip, Dead-eye instantly fired over Lorrimer's shoulder, cutting the terrorist down while Lorrimer was still taking aim.

'Shit,' Lorrimer acknowledged, 'either I'm getting old before my time or you're a phenomenon.'

'I'm pretty good,' Dead-eye said.

Lorrimer roared with laughter and slapped Dead-eye on the shoulder, though he knew that he had just been beaten at his own game. Thereafter he treated the young with the kind of respect he usually reserved only for veterans as old and experienced as himself.

'The kid's a natural,' he said privately to Abang.

'A born killer,' Abang said.

Just after last light on their final evening in the *ulu* they came across an encampment of guerrillas who seemed surprisingly unconcerned about guarding themselves. When Lorrimer looked closer, he noticed that the few guerrillas not sleeping were smoking from what could only be opium pipes.

'*Is* it opium?' he asked Abang in a whisper.

Abang nodded his confirmation. 'Look,' he said, pointing to the guerrilla's messy lean-tos. 'They are living in squalor. That suggests they are not CT, but renegade guerrillas, now living as outlaws –

the kind who rape and pillage in the name of Communism.' Abang pointed at the guerrillas' women, all of whom were equally slovenly, and either drunk on *samsu* or drugged from constantly smoking opium. 'Those women are not trained CT. They're just jungle whores. The men are *orang jahat* – bad men. We should neutralize them.'

'Then let's do it,' Lorrimer said.

The few bandits still awake, though unguarded, were surrounded by weapons which they would doubtless use if disturbed. Lorrimer therefore decided to disturb them permanently by blowing them to Kingdom Come. For this purpose he used another home-made bomb, lobbing it high to ensure that it fell close to the lean-to. It bounced into the soft earth near one of the men smoking opium. He removed the pipe from his lips, stared uncomprehendingly at the bomb, and was turning his head lazily, in an opium daze, to gaze questioningly at the others when the bomb exploded with a thunderous clap. It caused a violent eruption of soil, loose leaves and smoke that blew the kneeling group apart and set fire to the collapsing roof and walls of the lean-to.

Even before the smoke had cleared away, Deadeye was firing at the shadowy figures crawling and screaming on the ground. He adjusted his aim by the lines of spurting soil stitched by the bullets.

When one of the bandits actually managed to raise himself to his knees, swinging a British tommy-gun up into the firing position, Sergeant Lorrimer nearly cut him in two with a couple of bursts from his Browning autoloader. The man quivered like a bowstring, appeared to bow politely, then fell face first into the leaf-covered earth beside the still-burning fire. Another burst from Lorrimer's autoloader blew the fire apart.

Running forward, Lorrimer, Dead-eye and Abang between them checked the state of the bandits, men and women. All except one were dead. The survivor, a woman, had lost half her face and was bleeding profusely and clearly dying. Leaning over her, Abang snapped in Mandarin: 'Ah Hoi! Baby Killer! Where is he?'

The woman opened her mouth to speak, but instead coughed up blood. When Abang had wiped the blood away with an oily rag, he repeated his question: 'Ah Hoi! Baby Killer! Where is he?'

The woman coughed more blood, this time mixed with phlegm, thus clearing her throat, and eventually managed to get the words out.

'Telok Anson,' she whispered.

She coughed blood for the third and final time, then closed her dazed eyes and died.

'The Telok Anson swamp,' Abang repeated to

Lorrimer and Dead-eye. 'That place is a nightmare.'

'Our work's finished here,' Lorrimer said.

After six long, hard weeks in the *ulu* with Abang, and having finally learnt where Ah Hoi, 'Baby Killer', was hiding with his guerrillas, Lorrimer decided that they had learnt all they needed to know there and should start back to the base camp as soon as possible.

The following day, they broke up their jungle hide-out, carefully hid all traces of their presence, then hiked back to Abang's village, where they used the PRC 319 to call in the chopper of Army Air Corps pilot Lieutenant Ellis.

When the familiar, green Sikorski S-55 Whirlwind arrived, Ellis could find no space to land, but he threw down a rope ladder and Lorrimer and Dead-eye – their loads a lot lighter than when they had arrived, but still heavily laden with packed bergens and weapons – waved goodbye to Abang and hauled themselves up the ladder.

The helicopter flew them back to the base camp in no time at all.

11

'What I learnt,' Sergeant Lorrimer told Captain Callaghan as they sat side by side in wicker chairs on the covered verandah of the base camp's timber-and-thatch administration building, 'is that once we've weeded out the last of the cowboys, we have to implement a completely different kind of training programme. We can attempt the basics of that programme here – trying it out, as it were – before we enter the Telok Anson swamp, but a proper, full-length programme can only be put into operation once we're back in England.'

'What kind of programme?' Callaghan asked.

'I'm thinking of something more extensive than standard military training. Some form of cross-training. What we need, I believe, are men who're particularly good at most kinds of military activity – weapons, battle strategy, teamwork, endurance – but also have specialist training in other areas that ensure they're ready for just about any kind of environment or physical challenge – heat, cold, jungle, mountain, rivers, the sea, the air – at least, with regard to the latter, parachute inserts, such as our tree-jumping.'

'The men already do that in a way. Certainly each member of the four-man teams is cross-trained in signals, demolition, medicine and basic languages.'

'Correct, but only since coming here. We have to make such training the *modus operandi* of the Regiment and implement the training back in England. The men have learned those subjects here almost by accident; picked up as and when necessary, but we should teach them in depth and expand the curriculum to include specialist techniques relating to survival in jungles and deserts, at sea and on snow-covered mountains, and of course in the air. What the men have learned here so far relates only to Malaya, which means they only have an expedient, basic knowledge of it. In future, they should be prepared for all contingencies and environments before they even leave the base in England. Combined with that, there should be a much more rigorous selection programme.'

'Are you doing a report on this?'

'Yes, boss.'

'I look forward to reading it, but give me a summary.'

'I'm thinking basically about a three-part selection and training programme. First is Selection. We only consider men with at least two years' service in another regiment and who, while being self-sufficient, will have no record of troublemaking and can still work well in a team. The selection will be based on a three-week training period tougher than any devised so far, concentrating on physical stamina and endurance, as well as determination and exceptional skills at map-reading and cross-country navigation. This will be followed by a week of rigorous mental and physical testing. Those who fail, even by injury, will be returned to their original units without recourse to appeal.'

'That's pretty rough,' Callaghan said.

'That's the idea,' Lorrimer replied. 'It will rid us at an early stage of those who're psychologically and physically unsuitable, leaving only the *crème de la crème*.'

'OK, what next?'

'Those passing Basic Training and Selection go on to a few months of further training – or Continuation Training as I've called it. This consists of patrol tactics for every conceivable situation and environment, including jungle, desert, mountain and sea; advanced signalling; demolition; first-aid and combat survival. Anyone failing at any point is RTU'd instantly.'

'Aye, aye, aye!' Callaghan whispered, shaking his right hand as if in agony. 'It hurts just to think of it, but what happens next?'

'The survivors . . .'

'Good word!'

'. . . go on to special, extensive jungle training, learning in detail everything we've learnt here in Malaya, preferably in a real jungle, followed by a static-line parachute course and a set number of actual jumps.'

'Still being RTU'd at any point if they don't come up to scratch.'

'Exactly.'

'And those passing are finally allowed to wear the beige beret and Winged Dagger badge.'

'Yes . . . but their training isn't over yet.'

'Lord have mercy! Continue.'

'Once badged, they go on to Cross-Training proper, including Escape and Evasion (E & E) and Resistance-to-Interrogation (R & I) exercises; High Altitude Low Opening, or HALO, insertion techniques; special boat skills for amphibious warfare and insertions; lessons in the driving and maintenance of every kind of military vehicle, including motor-bikes; and Close Quarters Battle (CQB) skills in a so-called 'killing house' designed just for that, with pop-up targets and false decoys; and, finally, fully comprehensive lessons in medicine and languages relevant to anywhere we might be sent in the next decade. By the time they finish that lot, your SAS troopers will be the finest in the world – and no bad apples.'

'Major Pryce-Jones will be pleased. He's already been talking about extensive Cross-Training, with all the men capable of doing all jobs, but some specializing in some more than the others. He's working on the possibility of dividing the four Sabre Squadrons of the Regiment into four 16-man troops, each of which, while manned by men with multi-skills, will have its own specialist role. So far he's thought of a Mobility Troop, specializing in operations in Land Rovers, fast-attack vehicles and motor-bikes; a Boat Troop, specializing in amphibious warfare and insertions; a Mountain Troop, specializing in mountain and Arctic warfare; and an Air Troop to be used for freefall parachuting, tree-jumping and HALO insertions. All of these men will, of course, be interchangeable as the need arises – so your ideas for a special SAS Selection and Training course should go down nicely with the OC.'

'Good.'

Even as they were talking, a distant growling in the sky announced the arrival of a four-engined Blackburn Beverley transport plane. As it appeared west of the base camp, bringing the fortnightly resups, a bunch of REME (Royal Electrical and Mechanical Engineers) men, all stripped to the waist and already sweating, but wearing shorts and jungle boots with rolled-down socks, piled into a Bedford van that had been parachuted in two weeks earlier. The van immediately roared into life and was driven out of the camp, heading for the smaller cleared area being used as a Drop Site. Less than a minute later the Beverley passed over the DS and began dropping supplies out of its rear door. The parachutes blossomed into white flowers that drifted down against the sheer blue sky towards the green canopy of the jungle.

'How was Dead-eye?' Callaghan asked.

'Perfect. A natural if ever I saw one. He made his first CT killing with a crossbow and didn't even flinch. I've never seen anything quite like. He's so nice otherwise.'

'A freak of nature,' Callaghan said. 'They're bound to pop up in this business. I'm glad he's on our side. I'm surprised, by the way, that you and Dead-eye lost so little weight.'

'That's because Abang taught us how to live properly off the jungle, which is what we've got to teach the men when back in England, and weed out the unsuitable. Any problems in that regard?'

Callaghan sighed. 'We've reason to believe that

Trooper Laughton, when making his way back during that field exercise in Penang, beat a Malay student unconscious, then stole his bicycle, cycled back to the base, dumped the bicycle just before reaching the main gates and walked the next few hundred yards back to the camp. The student has since lodged a protest and we've been forced to deny that it was one of our men. But some locals saw Laughton on the student's bicycle shortly after the beating, so naturally we weren't given an easy ride. Laughton's best pal, Trooper Welsh, isn't much better.'

'Oh? What makes you say that?'

'You're not going to believe it.'

'Try me, boss.'

Callaghan had trouble keeping back his grin. 'The night before you left for the interior with Dead-eye, Pete Welsh was, reportedly, lying on his bed in the spider, deep in drunken slumber, with an erection that nearly went through the ceiling.'

Sergeant Lorrimer burst out laughing. 'Yes,' he said, when he'd settled down, 'I remember it well. He had that erection even as I was talking to Dead-eye.'

'Then obviously you missed the best part,' Callaghan said.

'Do tell.'

Callaghan chuckled, shaking his head in disbelief. 'Apparently Dennis the Menace and Boney Maronie entered the barracks and saw Pete Welsh's whopper of an erection. Knowing that Welsh had no sense of humour, Dennis the Menace got a pink ribbon – don't ask me where – and wrapped it around the tip of Welsh's erection, then tied it in a big bow. Welsh was so deep in drunken slumber he didn't even wake up. Boney Maronie then got out his camera and took a couple of nice Kodacolor pictures of the erection wearing its big pink-ribbon bow, making sure that Welsh could also be recognized. When the pictures were developed, he pinned them up in the mess hall for every man in the camp to see when he came in for his scran.'

Callaghan had to stop talking until Lorrimer got over his fit of laughter.

'Can I continue?' Callaghan asked.

'Yes, boss.'

'When Welsh entered the mess to a round of applause, then saw the candid photos of himself, he guessed immediately who'd done it and went for Dennis the Menace. A riot ensued. The mess was taken apart. Amazingly, Dennis the Menace, who's only half the size of Welsh, beat the blazes out of the latter, but not until the mess was half demolished. Eventually, they were separated, with Welsh made to stay a few days in the barracks of the Royal Marine Commandos. He is, however, now back in the SAS spider, though we've only managed to keep him apart from Dennis the Menace and Boney Maronie by sending them out on separate jungle patrols. It's funny, I know . . . – ' Callaghan saw the big grin on Lorrimer's pink face – 'but it's also a further indication that we need a more disciplined bunch of men than those we have here.'

'Which just goes to prove what I'm saying,' Lorrimer replied. 'We need a much tougher selection and training programme to ensure that only the cream of the crop get into the Regiment – and the programme I'm suggesting will do just that.'

'I think you're right,' Callaghan said. 'In the meantime, we'll have to go on keeping these bastards busy by giving them as much jungle training as we can possibly manage – of the kind you've just described – before we send them into that swamp to take out Ah Hoi.'

'I'll second that motion,' Lorrimer said. 'Just let me at them.'

'Go to it, Sarge.'

Lorrimer went at it. For the next ten days the men were put through a punishing routine of daily training that would prepare them for the Telok Anson swamp. Basing the training very much on what he and Dead-eye had learned from Abang during their own sojourn in the *ulu*, Lorrimer concentrated on jungle tracking, living off the land, primitive medicine, the construction of shelters, silent killing techniques, Standard Operating Procedures (SOPs) designed specially for the *ulu*, raft building and manoeuvring, and basic phrases in Mandarin and Malay, the former for communication with the CT, the latter to aid the campaign to win the 'hearts and minds' of the Sakai and Malay *ulu* dwellers. All of this was in addition to their normal military training in weapons maintenance and firing, camouflage, Close Quarters Battle, hand-to-hand fighting, tree-jumping and abseiling.

The training lasted from first to last light each day, with minimal breaks in between, the longest being the forty minutes allocated for a packed lunch. By the time the men had finished their evening meal in the mess back in the base camp, it was time to hit their bashas for a brief, usually sweaty and restless sleep. Nevertheless, though all this was demanding enough, other aspects of the course caused even more concern.

'I can't even *touch* a snake,' Dennis the Menace complained, studying the piece of skinned, boiled snake on the pointed end of his fork, 'let alone eat one of the fuckers! Who wants my share?'

'Sorry, can't help you,' Boney Maronie said, looking dubiously into the steaming pot he was stirring in the temporary camp they had made in the jungle just outside the base camp. 'I'm too busy trying to digest this stew composed of the meat of a constipated monkey and various herbs, leaves and vines from the *ulu*. It looks a lot better than it smells, but my lips remain sealed.'

'Eat it,' Dead-eye told him. 'It's OK, believe me. I had it myself lots of times and it was really quite good.'

'West Croydon,' Dennis the Menace said, tentatively nibbling at his cooked snake. 'That's where this poor unfortunate comes from and we all know what that means. They'd eat the fucking carpet off the floor, the poor sods are so poor.'

Boney Maronie burst out laughing. 'Christ, man,' he said, watching Dennis the Menace nervously sinking his teeth into his piece of hot snake, 'you look like you're being forced to suck cock. Just take a good fucking bite, man!'

'I'll take a good bite of this if you take a decent swallow of that soup. Come on, big mouth, let's see you!'

'I'm just waiting for it to cool down,' Boney Maronie said. 'That's all that's holding me back, mate.'

'*Hey, you two*!' Sergeant Lorrimer bawled, emerging from the head-high grass beside the river they had just come along on their imperfect bamboo rafts. 'What the hell are you doing sniffing around that scran like we've got all fucking day? Eat the food you cooked – eat it all – or deal with me. Get it?'

'Yes, boss!' Dennis the Menace and Boney Maronie chanted in unison.

'And swop,' Lorrimer told them. 'Dennis the Menace has some soup and Boney Maronie has some snake, and if any of you throw it back up you'll get my boot up your arse. *Eat, damn it! EAT!*'

The two troopers bolted down their food and didn't find it half bad, though both later confessed that they had felt a little queasy.

'A purely psychological reaction,' Dennis the Menace said later, as they poled their home-made rafts down the river, balanced precariously. 'It was no more than that.'

'As psychological as my nausea when this fucking raft rolls from side to side,' Boney Maronie replied, awkwardly handling the paddle rudder, located just behind Dennis. 'I feel sick each time this river turns rough.'

'Rough?' Dead-eye said, surprised. 'This river never does more than ripple!'

'Those aren't ripples, Dead-eye. They're fucking great waves.'

'Where? I don't see any waves?'

'That doesn't matter a shit.' Boney Maronie worked the rudder, heading in towards the river bank. 'It's all psychological, after all. If I feel waves, there *are* waves.' He manoeuvred the raft into the high, muddy bank, allowing the other men to gratefully pile off and return to the temporary camp to have a brew-up. 'And that river, believe me, was fucking rough. That's why I felt seasick.'

'What bullshit!' Pete Welsh said later, when he overheard Boney Maronie discussing the perils of river navigation. Welsh was on his knees in the small clearing near the river, finishing off his jungle lean-to. Stripped to the waist and pouring sweat, he looked like he'd been swimming. 'An arse-hole like you, mate – you probably get seasick playing with your toy duck in the bath.'

'My duck's bigger than yours, chum, which makes it worth playing with.'

Welsh laughed at that, though he still didn't feel too friendly. Since the riot in the mess hall, after he had seen the photos of the pink ribbon on his manhood, he had kept a fair distance from both Dennis the Menace and Boney Maronie. The tension was still there, bubbling under the surface, but right now he was grinning in that way that made him seem decidedly crazy.

'Oh, yeah!' he said. 'Right!'

'How's the lean-to going?' Sergeant Lorrimer asked, stepping out of nowhere as usual and looking red-faced.

'Fine, boss,' Welsh replied.

'It doesn't look fine to me. A bloody breeze, never mind a *Sumatras*, would blow that rubbish away.' Lorrimer walked up to the shelter that Welsh had spent three hours building and kicked one of the bamboo struts away, making the whole thing collapse. 'See?' he said, as Welsh's sweaty face turned purple with rage. 'A passing rat could have knocked that garbage over. Start building again.'

'I could kill that bastard,' Laughton said later to Welsh as the latter, still flushed with anger, laboriously rebuilt his jungle basha.

'Surprise, surprise,' Welsh replied sarcastically. 'What's got *you* going?

Laughton knelt on the leafy ground beside Welsh. 'I'm tracking through the *ulu*, right? I've been at it for five hours. Up and down hills that were practically vertical, across rock-strewn rivers, through snake-infested swamps, taking care to cover all my own tracks. Suffocating in the heat, sweating like a pig. Not a second's break, not a drink, not a smoko; just going like the clappers and obviously catching up on them, about half an hour to the RV. Then – would you believe it? – that bastard Lorrimer comes out of nowhere – just parts the fucking foliage and steps out like an elephant – and bellows: 'You dumb bastard! You've just torn off a twig and broken a spider's web, letting any halfwit follow your trail. You're going to be fined for this, Trooper, so you might as well turn back.' Half an hour to the RV! Can you fucking believe it?'

'Did you have a weapon with you?'

'M1 carbine.'

'Should have used it and blamed it on the CT. Shut that bastard up proper.'

'Christ, Pete, you sound like you mean that.'

Welsh just laughed manically.

They were made to spend nights sleeping in the *ulu*, under their temporary bashas, first shaking out their kit to check for creepy-crawlies, then covering themselves in mud to keep off the clouds of noisily whining insects, then listening to the unholy roar of the jungle's nocturnal chorus, and always whispering the kind of bitter complaints that actually expressed pride.

'Fucking Mandarin and Malay!' Dennis the Menace complained in a resounding whisper from his bivi-bag, stretched out beside Boney Maronie under their basha of bamboo, *atap* and rattan.

'It'd be easier to learn Swahili from a retarded deaf-mute born in Lapland. I mean, why do we have to learn *their* bloody language? They all speak English anyway.'

'Not here, they don't.' Boney was being philosophical. 'This is the *ulu*, mate, the *real* jungle – not bloody Singapore – and most of the prats here have never been to school, let alone learnt decent English. Of course, I don't mind the language classes myself, being pretty good at it.'

'Hey, Dead-eye, you hear that?' Dennis the Menace was outraged. 'Boney Maronie, who can't order a Tiger beer in a Chinese bar, thinks he's fluent in Chinese and Malay. Am I dreaming, or what?'

'He didn't say "fluent", Dennis.'

'He *implied* it,' Dennis insisted.

'I only said . . .'

'Bullshit!' Dennis the Menace said. 'That's bloody nonsense, Boney. I don't give a bugger what you say, you can't speak Chinese for shit. As for Malay – well, I don't care what you say, mate, I've heard you trying to speak it in those classes and it's just embarrassing. Isn't that right, Dead-eye?'

'Well, I . . .'

'See? Dead-eye agrees with me! What more can you say? Nothing! Not a damned thing! Just put a plug in it, Boney!'

196

'I don't think he has to,' Dead-eye said. 'I think he's sleeping already.'

'Fucking berk!' Dennis the Menace said.

The training continued.

After a fortnight of what many of them described proudly as 'Hell on earth' they were called to the briefing room in the bamboo-and-thatch HQ and informed by Captain Callaghan that the training had ended and they were about to go on a very important op. The men burst into applause.

'All right, all right!' Callaghan said, waving his hands to silence them. 'I'm delighted that you're delighted. But calm down and let me get on with this briefing.'

'With you, boss!' Dennis the Menace called out.

'Just let us loose!' Boney Maronie bawled.

'*Shut your mouths,*' Sergeant Lorrimer bellowed, 'and let the boss speak!'

That shut them all up.

'The reason you've had such intensive jungle training,' Callaghan said, 'is that tomorrow we're going into the Telok Anson swamp to take out the CT leader, Ah Hoi, also known as "Baby Killer", and his gang of guerrillas.'

The men cheered again, but were soon silenced by the red-faced glare of Sergeant Lorrimer.

'Getting rid of Ah Hoi is very important,' Callaghan said, 'and a little background may explain why.'

'No explanations required, boss,' Welsh said. 'Just let us at him.'

'Anyone ask you to speak, Trooper?' Lorrimer asked.

'No, Sarge.'

'To date,' Callaghan continued, 'we've managed to kill, capture or forced to surrender over 9,000 CT, leaving only a hard core of about two thou' still in the jungle. Because of our hearts-and-minds campaign, those remaining have lost the support of the aboriginals and other village communities. Realizing that they can no longer rule even a single region, the CT still left are widely scattered into groups whose only recourse is savage terrorism without any political objective. They are therefore in a greatly weakened position and should be relatively easy to capture or wipe out.'

'We've heard *that* one before,' Laughton said.

'One more word out of you, Trooper,' Lorrimer said, 'and I'll beat you so hard around the ears you'll be deaf for the rest of your worthless life.'

'Hear you loud and clear,' Laughton replied.

'The most influential of the numerous CT leaders,' Callaghan continued, as if such interruptions were perfectly normal, 'is Ah Hoi, whose disembowelment of a pregnant woman in front of her husband, a headman, and his villagers was merely the first in a long line of increasingly hideous atrocities that have succeeded in terrifying the aboriginals into doing anything he demands of them. For that very reason, we have to get rid of him.'

'Do you dick-heads understand that?' Lorrimer asked in a calmer voice.

'Yes, Sarge!' the men responded in unison.

'Good,' Lorrimer said, then turned to Callaghan. 'OK, boss, continue.'

'Presently,' Callaghan went on, trying to hide his smile, 'Ah Hoi and his guerrillas, being located little over a day's march through rubber plantations from Kuala Lumpur, are emerging regularly from the *ulu* to murder and pillage. Apart from the sheer horror of many of their atrocities, they're damaging us by causing too many of our Security Forces to be tied up in guard duties around the plantations. Our task, therefore, is to enter the Telok Anson swamp and bring out that murderous bastard and his men.'

There was a brief, thoughtful silence, until Deadeye asked: 'What's the swamp like?'

'Swamp-like.' Everyone laughed, but then Callaghan became serious. 'Approximately 18 miles by 9 miles – about the size of central London. Dense jungle, a maze of rust-brown water, mangroves and glutinous mud. Lots of rain and heat combined, making for dreadful humidity. Leeches galore. Every kind of bug, insect, and venomous creepy-crawly known to man. I'm sure you'll enjoy it.'

'How do we insert?' Boney Maronie asked.

'A secret parachute drop from a Beverley to the jungle canopy 3 miles west of the swamp. After the tree-jump, we march east into the swamp itself. Once in the swamp, we'll be waist deep in water all day and sleeping by night in hammocks or on improvised rafts. Now you know why you've been worked so relentlessly over the past two weeks.'

'We insert by Beverley?' Dennis the Menace asked.

'Yes. You'll be choppered back to Johore tomorrow morning, then flown in a Beverley back to the jungle in the afternoon. You won't have time for any fun in Johore, so don't even think of it. You touch down and take off again.'

'Gee, boss, you're so kind,' Welsh said.

'The Irish are an emotional race,' Callaghan said, 'so you're lucky to have me. Are there any more questions?' The silence was resolute. 'Right,' Callaghan said. 'We rise at first light, have breakfast, get kitted out, then get lifted off

in sticks of ten, which should take all morning.
Once in Johore, we transfer to the Beverleys and
fly on to the DZ. As I'm coming with you I won't
wish you good luck. Thank you, gentlemen. Class
dismissed.'

Obviously pleased that the bullshit was over
and the real work about to begin, the troopers
pushed their chairs back and hurried out of the
briefing room.

'About time!' Dead-eye whispered.

He couldn't wait to get stuck in.

12

The thirty-seven men selected to go into the swamp rose at first light, jolted themselves awake with a quick shower, put on their OGs, jungle boots and soft green bush hats, then went to the mess for an early breakfast, during which the confidence-boosting bullshit flew thick and fast.

The banter continued as they were marched by Sergeant Lorrimer to the quartermaster's stores and armoury, located mercifully in the shade of a copse of papaya palms. There, in groups of ten, they picked up, along with their usual kit, special waterproof jungle bergens, cosmetic 'cam' cream, dulling paint and strips of camouflage cloth for their weapons, lengths of para-cord to replace their weapons' standard-issue sling swivels, a plentiful supply of Paludrine, salt tablets, sterilization tablets, and a Millbank bag to filter water.

From the quartermaster's stores the first group marched the few yards to the armoury where, since they already had their personal weapons, they picked up additional fire-power, including L4A4s with curved 300-round box magazines of .303-inch bullets, fragmentation and smoke grenades, magazines of tracer bullets, flares, a couple of crossbows with lightweight alloy bolts and arrows, and some air rifles that fired darts instead of bullets. These were complemented by 5.56mm M16 assault rifles with attachments, including bayonet, bipod, telescopic sights, night-vision aids, 40mm M203 clip-on grenade-launchers, and 40mm grenades for the launcher, including smoke, HE and phosphorus.

When the weapons had been collected, the ten men moved along to the radio store where they signed for their PRC 320 radio sets, one for each of the four- or five-man teams, plus lightweight, hand-powered generators to recharge the batteries and spare compact batteries for emergencies. Finally, each man collected his Irvin X-Type model parachute.

Returning to the spider, already sweating from humping their heavy gear, the men packed their kit and camouflaged their weapons with quick-drying green paint. When the final task, camouflaging themselves, was complete, they made their way, heavily burdened, to the helicopter landing pad, where the familiar face of Lieutenant Ralph Ellis greeted them. The Army Air Corps pilot was preparing his beloved Sikorski S-55 Whirlwind for take-off.

'Morning, ladies,' Ellis said, taking note of the camouflage make-up. 'Nice to see you all looking so pretty for our nice Sunday outing.' When the anticipated ribaldry had subsided, the pilot continued: 'I'll be lifting you off in sticks of ten, which will take four flights, so you're all going to have to be patient. Given the time required for lift-off, flight, putting down and return flight, I'd estimate no later than noon to have you all on the ground at Johore. OK, in you go.'

The first ten, including Callaghan, clambered into the chopper and took their seats with some difficulty, hampered by the sheer bulk of their combined bergens, parachutes, weapons and other kit.

'Bit cramped in here, boss,' Dennis the Menace said as he adjusted the straps of his parachute pack and bergen so that he could actually sit on the seat. 'Not exactly first class.'

'If I had first-class passengers,' Ellis replied, 'I'd try to improve things – but you know how it is.'

Dennis gave a hollow laugh.

'Where's Sergeant Lorrimer?' Laughton asked. 'Still snoring his head off in his basha?'

'He's still at the armoury,' Callaghan explained, 'and will leave with the last batch of men. I know you can't live without him, Laughton, but I'm sure you can wait.'

'For ever,' Welsh said.

'Have you men all settled in?' the Loadmaster enquired. 'We're about to take off.'

'Let us pray,' Boney Maronie said.

The sudden roaring of the Whirlwind's Wright R-1300 800-hp engine put a stop to any further conversation. The noise increased when the props started spinning, creating a whirlwind of fine soil, loose leaves and seedlings. The chopper lifted off the ground, swayed briefly from side to side, rose vertically to an altitude of about 1,500 feet, then flew horizontally towards Johore.

Suddenly, the vast canopy of the jungle was spread out below, an alluvial green sea, with the sun rising above the eastern horizon like a great silvery bowl.

It was a spectacular flight, but it took only thirty minutes, then the base camp came into view, rapidly spreading out below them, with its wood-and-thatch buildings encased in the cleared jungle clearly outlined from the sky by a great rectangle of coconut palms, papaya trees and inky-dark monsoon drains.

As the Whirlwind descended the men could make out the latrines, open showers, a motor pool packed with Bedford trucks and Jeeps, and an airstrip lined with Valetta and Beverley transports, as well as Whirlwind, Dragonfly and Sycamore helicopters. It looked like a busy base.

When the chopper touched down, the troopers piled out and gathered together just beyond the pull of the slipstream whipped up by the props, which were still spinning, though in neutral and slowing down. When Ellis cut the engine, the props gradually stopped turning and a refuelling tanker, which he had called up by radio, came across the airstrip to fill up the Whirlwind's tanks, enabling him to take off again.

Feeling hot and sweaty already, Dennis the Menace and Boney Maronie started slipping off their parachute packs and bergens, in order to rest on the grassy verge at the edge of the tarmac.

'Something wrong with you, gentlemen?' Captain Callaghan asked them.

'Sorry, boss,' Dennis replied. 'What's that?'

'Why are you sitting down? Are you feeling ill?'

'Well, no, boss . . .' Dennis glanced at Boney Maronie. 'We're just waiting for the others to arrive. I mean . . .'

'So you thought you'd sit on your fat arses twiddling your thumbs. Well, lads, you won't. Get those parachutes and bergens back on your shoulders, pick up your kit, and follow me across the airstrip to the Beverley. You can pass the time by putting your kit on the plane and then helping the Loadmaster with the supplies. OK? On your feet!'

With much moaning and groaning the men did as they were told, humping the parachute packs and bergens on to their backs, then following Callaghan across the sunbaked airstrip to where the RAF Beverley was being prepared for its flight to Telok Anson, south-west of Ipoh.

'Flight-Sergeant Norton?' Callaghan asked of the big man who was standing by the open boom door at the rear of the aircraft, wearing shorts, with rubber flip-flops on his feet. Stripped to the waist, he was gleaming with sweat and supervising the loading being done by a bunch of Chinese coolies.

'Yes, sir,' the man replied, sounding as if he'd smoked too many cigarettes. 'Flight-Sergeant Norton. That's me.'

'This is the first batch of troopers for the parachute jump into Telok Anson. They can load their own kit and then give you any other help you need.'

'That might speed things up,' Norton said, smiling at the troopers. 'OK, you men, clamber up here and make your way through to the passenger hold. When you've dumped your gear, come back and see me and I'll keep you busy.'

'You're too kind,' Boney Maronie said.

'Heart of gold,' Norton replied. 'Now get your lazy arses on this aircraft and let's see some work done.'

With the help of the reluctant, moaning SAS troopers the coolies were able to complete the loading of the supplies a lot sooner than expected, which allowed everyone to have an early break. When the SAS men had been picked up in a Bedford and driven back to their quarters, the coolies were finally allowed to sit on the grassy verge to await the arrival of the next stick of ten men.

'We've been in that FOB for less than two months,' Welsh said, 'but it seems *years* since we passed through *this* hole. It's changed a lot since we left.'

'Yeah,' Laughton agreed, squinting against the dazzling sunlight as he gazed across the airstrip, past the parked aircraft and helicopters, to the sports ground, row of barracks and line of jungle at the other side. 'It's become a regular Piccadilly Circus – a helluva lot of movement and noise.'

This was true enough. Valettas, other Beverleys, and a variety of helicopters – Whirlwinds, Dragonflys and Sycamores – were taking off and landing at regular intervals, creating huge clouds of swirling dust and debris. Bedford trucks and jeeps were racing along the roads of the base, transporting troops and supplies. A squadron of Gurkhas was engaged in rifle drill on the sports area. The wired perimeter was being patrolled by Kampong Guards from the Malaya Police, while the guardhouses were manned by RAF MPs and covered by the Royal Marines manning the Bren guns and 3-inch mortars in the sangars on either side of the gates.

'All it needs is a brothel,' Boney Maronie said, 'filled with nice girls from George Town.'

'If they were nice girls they wouldn't work in a brothel,' Dennis the Menace pointed out. 'Though that fact isn't likely to put *you* off, mate.'

'I just follow my God-given instincts. What's wrong with that?'

'You haven't followed them for weeks,' Welsh said. 'Nor has anyone else. I can take everything they throw at me in this filthy hole, except being deprived of my bit of tail.'

'I can't remember what a bit of tail looks like,' Dennis the Menace confessed.

'Since there's no brothel here, that's academic,' Laughton observed. 'Christ!' he added as an afterthought. 'I feel horny all of a sudden! Stop talking about it.'

The morning passed slowly, with the sun growing

stronger. Lolling about on the grass, the men began to feel soporific. Eventually, however, two more sticks of ten men and the final stick of seven, including Sergeant Lorrimer and Trooper 'Deadeye' Parker, were brought in on three separate flights of the Whirlwind. By then it was just after noon and ferociously hot.

The men took their places in the Beverley and the aircraft took off. As a Beverley can carry 70 parachutists at a time, the 37 SAS paratroopers were all going to make the jump at the same time. It was a blessing that the flight took only thirty minutes, as the interior of the aircraft was suffocatingly hot and humid at that time of day. The men were therefore relieved when Norton opened the port and starboard doors, as well as the large boom door, letting cooler air come rushing in.

'OK, men,' Captain Callaghan said, standing up and adjusting the straps of his combined parachute pack and strapped-on bergen. 'I'll be going out first as the drifter. You men will follow on the command of Flight-Sergeant Norton. You'll go out in sticks of four from the port and starboard doors, and left and right of the boom door. The DZ is located in the bush about 12 miles from the edge of the swamp. The supplies will be dropped in the same area. Once we've collected and shared out the supplies, we'll march east and enter the swamp.'

'*Action stations*!' Flight-Sergeant Norton bawled.

'OK, men,' Callaghan said briskly. 'Stand up.' When the men had done so, he sorted them into four queues of nine men each, each lined up at one of the four chosen exits. He then took his position at the big boom door, holding onto the side and waiting for the overhead green light to flash. Looking down he saw the brilliant-green jungle canopy, stretching out to the curved line of the sheer blue horizon. It seemed like a long way down.

'Right!' Norton bawled and tapped him on the shoulder.

Callaghan threw himself out, was swept away on the roaring slipstream, escaped and started dropping like a stone, then tugged on the parachute cord. He was jerked back up, swung like a pendulum, then started drifting down towards the jungle, through a silence only broken by the wind whipping under the parachute. Though heavily burdened with his parachute back-pack, bergen, bandoliers and weapons, he felt as light as a feather.

As the jungle canopy came up towards him, gaining light and shade and dimension, he saw the relatively clear area of stunted grass and bush designated as the DZ, and using the lines of his chute, steered himself in that direction. Shaken by a gust of wind, he saw the treetops suddenly racing up towards him. He steered himself to the west, missed the dense, dangerous canopy, then plunged down a deep well of blurred greenery on to grass-covered earth.

When his feet hit the ground, he let his legs buckle, then rolled over with the parachute tugging at him. He reined the lines in, then popped the chute, feeling a sense of freedom when it broke loose from his bergen. At that point he stopped rolling.

Looking up, he saw the Beverley circling high above, dull grey against the blue sky, with sticks of men spilling out in four different directions and plunging towards the chutes billowing open below him. Before the last men reached the first batch, their own opening chute would pull them back up, then let them drift down above the others. It all looked rather beautiful.

The first men started landing in the bush around Callaghan, some having a clear fall, others tumbling down through the branches of the trees, still others snagged in the branches and uncoiling their knotted ropes to abseil the rest of the way down.

Callaghan wrapped up his chute, buried it in

the undergrowth, then, holding his Owen sub-machine-gun at the ready, went to join the men landing nearest to him.

The supplies, also being parachuted down, were falling over a fairly wide area, but well within the expected circular range.

As Callaghan hurried across the bush towards the nearest men, he saw one of those still coming down smashing brutally into the treetops. Caught by his own webbing, he was flipped over like a rag doll, smashed backwards into another thick branch, screamed in agony, then fell when the canopy collapsed. He bounced off more branches, smashed noisily through others, and eventually landed with a thud on his back – after a fall of over 100 feet. When he tried to call for help, the words came out as a shuddering, breathless wail of pain that did not sound human.

Callaghan turned around and headed in that direction, followed by some of the other grounded troopers. When they reached the man, it was immediately clear that he had seriously damaged his spine and was unable to move himself below the waist.

'Medic!' Dennis the Menace bawled.

Luckily, most of the men had landed already and a medic was among them. Responding promptly to the call, he checked the man's reactions, soon saw that he could feel nothing in his lower half and turned to whisper to Callaghan that he had broken his back.

'He has to be casevacked,' the medic said. 'This man can't be carried.'

'Damn!' Callaghan whispered.

Dead-eye, meanwhile, having fallen wide of the DZ and into the jungle canopy, found himself once more dangling by his parachute harness from one of the stronger branches of a tree. In fact, his fall had been stopped only 15 feet from the ground. Unable to shake the harness free, he released the bergen from the parachute back-pack and let it fall, rattling and banging its way down through the branches before hitting the soft carpet of leaves. Dead-eye was then able to wriggle out of the harness, freeing first one arm, then the other, and balancing himself precariously on the thick branch upon which he found himself sitting.

He was just about to lower himself to the ground when some bushes parted and a Chinese-looking man, obviously attracted by the noise of the falling bergen, entered the small clearing below. In his mid-twenties, he was barefoot and wearing khaki shorts, a shirt and military cap. And he was holding a British tommy-gun. He advanced on the tree, then stopped to stare down at the bergen. When he saw what it was, he froze on the spot, then glanced left and right, behind him and to the front. Then he knelt to examine the bergen.

Dead-eye was about to remove his 9mm Browning High Power handgun from its holster when he checked himself, for the sound of the shot would alert any other CTs in the vicinity. Changing his mind and moving as quietly as possible, he unsheathed his Fairburn-Sykes commando knife, gripped it tightly in his right hand, took a deep breath, then let himself slide off the thick branch and drop to the jungle floor.

He landed right beside the guerrilla, sliding his left arm around him as he did so, pulling him off his feet, and slashing the blade of the knife across his throat even as they both fell backwards into the leaves. The man could make no sound as his vocal cords had been cut, but he frantically kicked his legs, shuddered like an epileptic, and soaked Dead-eye's right hand in blood before gargling, choking and, after what seemed like an eternity, breathing his last.

Dead-eye slithered out from under him, checked that he was dead, closed and sheathed the commando knife, then picked his kit off the forest floor, slipped the straps of the heavy bergen over his shoulders, tightened them and checked all the weapons. Satisfied that everything was in order, he hurried off through the jungle, towards the clearing where the DZ was located and where most of the other men had dropped successfully.

Most, but not all. When Dead-eye arrived in the thinner forest of the bush, he found the squadron already engaged in the task of creating a temporary LZ for a helicopter.

'What's going on?' he asked Boney Maronie.

'Trooper Clayton broke his back when landing and is going to be casevacked back to Johore.'

'He didn't get far,' Dead-eye said.

'Where on earth did *you* land?' Captain Callaghan asked.

'Over there,' Dead-eye replied, waving his hand to indicate the nearby jungle. 'I got stuck halfway down a tree, but directly above an armed guerrilla. But don't worry, boss. I handled the situation.'

'You neutralized him?'

'Yes, boss.'

'Are you sure he was a guerrilla?' Callaghan asked.

'Absolutely. He was Chinese, wore one of those military caps, and was carrying a British tommy-gun.'

Sergeant Lorrimer had joined them to listen in on the conversation. When Dead-eye had finished talking, Lorrimer glanced automatically at the jungle.

'Well, well,' he said. 'We've had contact already.

216

Do you think there are any more in that bit of jungle?'

'No, I don't think so, Sarge. I made a hell of a racket coming down, yet that guerrilla was the only one to appear. I think he was some kind of point man, just looking around. The rest are probably still in the swamp.'

'Let's hope so,' Lorrimer said. He turned away to speak to Alf Laughton, who was in charge of a radio set. 'Did you manage to get in contact with Johore?'

'Yes, Sarge. The chopper's on its way and should be here any minute now.'

'Excellent.' Lorrimer turned back to Dead-eye. 'Since you've been a good boy, you can take your pick: either help clear an LZ for that chopper or give a hand with bringing in the supplies.'

'I'll bring in the supplies.'

'Go to it, kid.'

While half of the men were using their *parangs* to hack a clearing large enough for the chopper to land, the other half spread out to bring in the crates scattered around the DZ. After smashing open the wooden crates and metal containers that had come down on parachutes, they piled the supplies in a heap just outside the area being cleared for the LZ, completing the job just as an RAF Sycamore search-and-rescue helicopter came in to pick up the casualty.

The clearing made so hastily in the bush was just enough to allow the helicopter's rotor blades to miss the surrounding foliage. But it was still impossible to land because of the swampy terrain. Nevertheless, in an impressive display of flying skill, the pilot brought the helicopter into the small clearing, its rotors virtually scraping the trees, and hovered just above the swampy ground, with one wheel resting on a log, while the casualty, now strapped to the stretcher, was loaded aboard. Less than a minute later, the helicopter lifted off again, soon vanishing beyond the canopy of trees, leaving an ominous silence in its wake.

The spare weapons, ammunition and supplies were distributed among the men; then, as heavily burdened as pack mules, they marched east, towards the beckoning nightmare of the Telok Anson swamp.

13

It looked normal at first. To get to the swamp they had to pass through the stretch of jungle where Dead-eye had despatched the lone guerrilla. The corpse would have looked peaceful had it not been for the ghastly mess of congealed blood around the slashed throat and the black clouds of flies that were frantically trying to feed off it. Though the instinctive reaction of everyone was to ignore the grisly scene, Callaghan ordered that the corpse be buried in case any other guerrillas were in the vicinity and might be tipped off, by the discovery of the dead man, to the presence of the SAS here in the swamp. Using *changkols*, or large hoes, previously purchased from the Sakai, a couple of the troopers soon scooped out a shallow grave, threw the dead guerrilla into it, replaced the soil, then sprinkled loose leaves over the ground to make it look the same as before. The patrol then moved on.

The first hour was easy, a casual stroll in

single file through the jungle, kicking up the loose leaves, feeling grateful for the shade. Then they reached the edge of the swamp and everything changed.

The trees seemed to close in upon them, behind them, in front of them, forming an impenetrable living wall that had to be hacked away with the *parangs*. The ground became more marshy, squelching underfoot, making walking more laborious and exhausting. After only thirty minutes in the swamp, the sky was blocked out, the air had become appallingly humid and, even worse, was filled with whining flies, mosquitoes, midges, flying beetles, the occasional hornet and other equally ravenous winged insects of a type the troopers had never seen before. They all attacked noisily, viciously and constantly, further distracting the men from what they were doing.

Soon the wet ground became even more marsh-like, turning to mud, slopping over their boots, soaking their trouser legs and giving the impression that it was trying to suck them down like quicksand. Walking became monstrously difficult and soon left most of them breathless.

Unlike the jungle, the swamp offered a constant chorus of croaking, squawking, clicking, drumming, and sudden, startling rustling in the undergrowth. The latter, in particular, made the men jumpy, even causing them to suddenly raise their weapons, ready to fire.

Within an hour, the mud had turned to rust-brown water that became deeper with every step they took. Three hours later, when every man was running with sweat, he was also soaked up to the hips with water and forced to hold his personal weapon either across his chest or above his head. Both positions placed tremendous strain on the arms, causing sharp pains to dart along them, from shoulder to wrist.

With the water came the leeches. Already the trek was leading them along river banks and through more muddy water, the depths of which varied from shin to neck-high. Those parts of the body that were submerged were the prey for fat swamp leeches, which, as most of the men now knew, could consume half a pint of blood before being detected. And then, as if to ensure that there would be no reprieve for the struggling men, when they came to high ground that brought them out of the water they instantly became the target for the malarial mosquito and other insects. Before long, even the toughest soldier was beginning to think he was in hell on earth.

Their trials were made no easier by the fact that they were not allowed to speak on the march for fear either that some lurking guerrilla might overhear them or that their own voices would hide the sounds of an approaching enemy. Using only sign language, they were forced in on themselves, and thus distracted even more by the sounds all around them, particularly the sudden, sharp rustling which indicated sudden movement in the undergrowth. Usually these were caused by snakes, jungle pigs, monkeys or rats as big as rabbits.

By mid-afternoon the heat and humidity were appalling, making them pour more sweat and feel nauseous or nearly suffocated. Combined with the constant gloom caused by the dense jungle canopy, the sticky, oppressive heat made them feel unreal, disorientated, less capable of coherent thought and quick reactions. This only made many of them more anxious about the unseen CTs and suspicious of every sound in the teeming undergrowth.

In that state, it was easy for them to imagine that the jungle had a life of its own and was deliberately tormenting them. This seemed to be particularly true when they emerged from a swampy area to what at first sight appeared to be relatively clear, dry ground. Invariably, however, this turned out to be *belukar*, or secondary jungle, with thickets of thorn, bracken and bamboo more impenetrable than ever and covered with *mengkuang*, a gargantuan leathery grass with pointed blades. In one hour of back-breaking work, they would cover a mere hundred yards.

Before nightfall, they looked for somewhere to lay up, but where the water was not a couple of feet deep, the ground was too marshy to be used. They therefore looked for an area where the trees were close enough, and strong enough, to hold hammocks. Sleeping in this manner, swaying precariously above the snake-infested water or mud, was not made any easier by the jungle's nocturnal racket, nor by the countless insects that buzzed and whined all night, diving repeatedly at the frustrated men to get at their sweat and blood. It was also impossible to get rid of the leeches that had clung to their bodies, beneath the clothes, when they were wading chest-deep in the water. A final bar to sleep was the constant fear, encouraged by the ceaseless rustling of the undergrowth, that snakes, poisonous spiders or other venomous creatures would drop on to them from the branches directly above.

The second day, given the men's state of exhaustion, proved even more difficult. Subsequent days, during which they found no trace of a terrorist, were worse still, because the deeper into the swamp they went, the more nightmarish it became.

Each day, from the steamy mists of dawn to the damp, chilling sunrise, they had to force their way through stinking mud, rotting vegetation and thorny branches, sometimes wading up to their necks in the marsh channels, at other times practically swimming across open water, under drooping coils of vine, rattan and giant, razor-sharp leaves which cut their arms and faces, so driving the insects into a feeding frenzy and giving the growing number of fat leeches even more blood to feed upon.

Within a couple of days each man smelt of the swamp, his rotting clothes adding to the general stench of the place and hanging ever more loosely on his shrinking frame. This loss of weight was made worse by the fact that they were unable to cook decent food in the swamp and so had to rely on their dry, tasteless, high-calorie rations.

Though none of them actually hallucinated, all of them were driven back into themselves and spent a lot of time blocking out the horrors they were going through with memories of where they had come from and what they held most dear.

Try as he might not to become too distracted, Captain Callaghan found himself yearning for the sunny hills of Sicily and Italy, where he had served with Special Raiding Squadron, the renamed 1 SAS, in 1943. The gloomier the jungle became, the more vividly Callaghan saw the sun-scorched plains of Enna; the filthier the swamp became, the more colourful became his recollections of the Adriatic coast and Anzio. Callaghan had enjoyed the war, even the unsuccessful raids, feeling only half alive during the immediate post-war years when he returned to No. 3 Commando and divided his time between his family – he had two teenage daughters – and the dreary routine of a peacetime Army. He had been very glad, therefore, to be posted to Malaya at the start of the Emergency, for he was revitalized by fighting in the jungle. Nevertheless, though he basically loved being here, this present murderous hike, in pursuit of an 'invisible' enemy, left him no recourse but to escape from the horrors of the swamp by recalling the sunnier climates he had fought in during the war.

Similarly, Sergeant Lorrimer often found himself recalling the wide, open spaces of the North African desert, where he had been one of the first members of the SAS to go out on patrol with the Long Range Desert Group. Lorrimer had loved the desert, with its silence and space and vast, open sky; completely different from this filthy swamp with its noise, humidity and constant gloom. Waist-deep in water, ducking low to avoid drooping vines, he consoled himself by reliving the many daring raids he and his fellow SAS troopers had made in jeeps against enemy airfields around Benghazi, Bagoush and Sidi Haneish. He also thought occasionally of his wife in their small house in Runcorn, Cheshire, and of his children, a boy and two girls, now all grown up and married; but what he most remembered, as he sweated and stank in this filthy swamp, was the feel of the wind against his face and the sun dazzling his vision, as the jeeps tore across the desert plains to hit another German airfield. Now, more than ever, he yearned to feel and see that again, but instead there was only suffocating humidity and unrelieved gloom.

Trooper Dennis 'the Menace' Dudbridge was thinking a lot about drinking bitter in his local in Bristol. Before joining the regular Army, he had worked as a labourer in the docks at Avonmouth, where the men liked rough fun and games, particularly drinking and fighting. Dennis had been a heavy drinker from the minute he first set foot in a pub. He had also been quick to use his fists, which accounted for his broken nose and scarred upper lip. Married at eighteen after getting his girlfriend pregnant, he had sired four more kids, found home life increasingly irksome, and finally decided to escape it by joining the Army. Transferred to the Gloucestershire Regiment after his basic training, he had thoroughly enjoyed being away from home and was even more pleased when posted to West Berlin. There, when not on pointless manoeuvres or on guard duty at the Wall, he had lived the life of a hard-drinking bachelor. This did not change when his tour of duty ended and he returned to England.

Never much of a womanizer, Dennis liked his beer, darts, and macho conversation, preferably in a noisy, smoky pub. As he disliked being at home, he was happy enough to be in Malaya, but he didn't like this filthy swamp one bit.

Corporal 'Boney Maronie' Malone blocked out the horrors of the swamp with visions of the various women he'd had since losing his virginity at the relatively late age of twenty-three. He had, however, made up for lost time by sampling as many women as possible since then. Now twenty-nine and still a single man, he wanted no more out of life than a bit of nooky, a fast car, plenty to eat and drink, and a fair amount of lawful adventure with the SAS.

He required this colourful way of life because his mother had died when he was five years old, his father was a decent, deeply religious but dried-up bookkeeper for a firm of accountants in Coventry, where Boney Maronie had been born and bred, and his whole childhood and adolescence in the cathedral city had been lonely and boring beyond belief.

Boney Maronie's need for the fast lane explained his love of the SAS; yet even he was having difficulty in maintaining his enthusiasm while dragging his feet through mud, wading chest-deep in water, breathing humid air and the stench of natural decay, fighting off crazed insects, and keeping on the alert for poisonous snakes, scorpions, centipedes, hornets and the even more dangerous CT. Boney attempted to maintain his enthusiasm and ignore the swamp's vileness by recalling the many women he had known and then reducing them in his fevered imagination to mere artefacts composed of sweat-slicked skin, heaving breasts, erect nipples, moist, pouting lips and long hair tangled beautifully across eyes luminous with lust. Even being eaten alive by mosquitoes and midges, Boney Maronie could get an erection that made him feel superhuman.

Alf Laughton kept going by pretending that any minute now they were going to be lifted out of the swamp and deposited in Penang, which he remembered so vividly, having been there in 1953 with the King's Own Yorkshire Light Infantry. Born in Birkenhead, Merseyside, one of the five children of married publicans who worked night and day, Laughton felt at home as one of a large group and perhaps had gravitated to the Army for that very reason. Receiving little parental affection and largely ignored by his brothers and sisters, he soon devised various ways of getting himself attention, which mainly meant creating mischief. An inveterate troublemaker at school, he was not much better when he went to work, which he did at fourteen, as an apprentice welder in the shipyard. Eventually fired for bad behaviour, including dangerous practical jokes, he enlisted in the regular Army, which guaranteed him a better time than he would have had doing his National Service.

Given his dreary background, it was perfectly natural that he should find life in the Army more satisfying than Civvy Street and his first posting overseas, to Butterworth, Malaya, was the most exotic experience he'd had to date. Spending most of his spare time in Penang, a brief ferry cruise across the Strait of Malacca, he soon came to love the place, with its trishaws, *sampans*, bars, brothels, bazaars, markets, and beautiful women in figure-hugging *cheongsams*. Depressed when his tour of duty was over and he had to return to England, he played one too many practical jokes on his fellow soldiers, had one too many drinks, got into one too many fights, and was encouraged to join the newly reformed SAS by an NCO sick of the sight of him.

Now, here he was, pleased to be back in Malaya, but not so pleased to be slogging through this dark, dank, mosquito-infested swamp. He therefore dreamt of being lifted out and set down in the exotic, familiar streets of Penang.

Laughton's mate, Trooper Pete Welsh, was keeping going by ignoring the filth and dangers of the swamp and dreaming of revenge against all those in the squadron who had slighted him or otherwise riled him. An illegitimate child, he had been raised in Finsbury Park, North London, where his prostitute mother worked the pubs and brought the men back to her squalid bedsit, earning her money while he looked on, learning the facts of life in the most direct, brutal way possible. An alcoholic who was often beaten up by her clients, his mother just as frequently took her revenge out on her son, leaving him black and blue, traumatized by grief and fear. She would then weep tears of drunken remorse and try to buy his forgiveness with the presents he never received on Christmas or for his birthdays.

Welsh had suffered all this quietly until he was conscripted, trained as an explosives expert and posted to No. 101 Special Training School, Singapore. From there he transferred to the 3rd Corp, where, with other Sappers, he harassed the Japanese by blowing up railroads and bridges of strategic importance.

Though an excellent soldier, he never settled down and exploded at the slightest provocation, having violent fights that landed him in the cells. Nevertheless, he loved what he was doing – the war turned him on – and so he decided to go straight from National Service into the regular Army. Informed by his NCOs that the most expedient way of doing this was by signing up for the recently reformed SAS, which was desperate for volunteers and not yet vetting them too closely, Welsh did just that and soon found himself back in Malaya.

So here he was, slogging through a swamp that most of the other men thought was a nightmare, though it was, to Welsh, merely another place where he could take his revenge on the world in general and Dennis the Menace in particular.

No way in the world would Welsh let someone tie a pink bow on his cock, much less take a photograph of it, to be pinned up on the notice board in the mess.

He would have his revenge.

Welsh's energy was fuelled by the rage he was secretly nurturing as he slogged through the filth of the swamp.

His time would come soon.

Adding to the increasing anger, despair and frustration of the men was their continuing lack of contact with the enemy. Frequently they came across camps recently vacated by the terrorists, but the guerrillas themselves were as invisible as most of the alien wildlife in the undergrowth.

'Ah Hoi knows he's being followed,' Callaghan told Lorrimer as they studied a site littered with the shells of turtles eaten by the terrorists. 'I think the casevac of Trooper Clayton must have alerted them to our presence here. Now they're keeping ahead of us.'

'Then we have to block off their escape,' Lorrimer replied.

'Exactly. I think I should get on the radio and ask for another squadron to be dropped east of the swamp, to form a cordon around the eastern perimeter, then move in towards us, catching the guerrillas in the middle.'

'Those bastards are like swamp rats,' Lorrimer replied, 'knowing every tree, every bend in every river, every way out. So I don't think that one squadron will be enough to keep them in, though a pincer movement will certainly help when it comes to finishing them off.'

'You think we need even more men?'

'I think we should ask for that squadron to be dropped east of the swamp as you suggested. At the same time, however, the whole swamp should be encircled by a military and police cordon, with barbed wire placed along the coast, to prevent

anyone coming in or out that way. Keep the
bastards trapped in here and, with that pincer
movement, we should trap them eventually.'

'Agreed,' Callaghan said. As Major Pryce-Jones
was now based in Johore, Callaghan asked Laughton
to get him on the blower. When the trooper had done
so, Callaghan made his request. After listening
attentively, he handed the microphone back to
Laughton. 'He's OK'd it,' he said to Lorrimer,
'but insists that it'll take another few days. Most
of the men are already out on jungle patrols around
Johore. But he's going to call in D squadron and
send them out as soon as they're organized, which
should be two days from now. In the meantime
we're to continue advancing towards the centre of
the swamp.'

'It's going to be one hell of a hike, Captain.'

'Who dares wins,' Callaghan said.

Their route across the swamp was taking them
alongside the Tengi River. Checking by the side of
the river, Dead-eye, now an expert tracker after
his training with Abang, noted a series of broken
branches and leaves directly over where footsteps
had been covered with leaves, indicating that some
men in bare feet had hiked east, obviously heading
for the centre of the swamp.

'The CT,' Lorrimer deduced. 'Ah Hoi's men.'

'Right,' Callaghan said. 'As we thought, they're

retreating back into the swamp, trying to cover their tracks.'

'Then let's follow them,' Dead-eye said.

'No,' Callaghan replied. 'This is a relatively dry area, so I think we should stay here for the night and move on in the morning. While we're setting up camp, you can go out alone and check if any CT are in the area. They can't be too far ahead of us now, but we don't want to run into them without warning. Ok, Dead-eye, get going.'

Because of his frail physique, Dead-eye, weighed down with a bergen that included full camping gear and an arsenal of spare grenades and ammunition, looked even more heavily burdened than the others. This impression was only emphasized by the fact that he was carrying a 5.56mm M1 assault rifle with the bayonet, telescopic sight and 40mm M203 grenade-launcher already fixed to it. Also, strapped down the back of his bergen, was the crossbow with a belt of lightweight alloy bolts and arrows. In fact, Dead-eye looked like a bizarre Quasimodo as he turned away and headed deeper into the jungle, leaving the rest of the squadron behind to fix up the camp.

'You go with him,' Callaghan said to the nearest trooper, Neil Moffatt. 'Keep his back covered.'

'Right, boss,' Moffatt said, picking up his Owen

sub-machine-gun and following Dead-eye into the jungle.

'OK, Sarge,' Callaghan said to Lorrimer, now confident that the CT were heading west and that it was safe to camp there. 'Tell the men to make up their bashas for the night. They can talk, wash themselves in the river and even have something to eat and drink. But they still can't light fires.'

'Right, boss, I'll tell them.'

Delighted to be given a break on what amounted to solid ground, instead of in mud or water, the men enthusiastically washed themselves in the river, ate their cold, high-calorie rations, then created their own personal style of basha. One made a root shelter by packing soil between the extended roots of a tree, thus turning it into a little cave. Another made a bough shelter by unrolling his bivi-bag under the outspread branches of a fallen tree, which formed a natural ceiling. A third made a sapling shelter by draping his waterproof poncho over a series of horseshoe-shaped branches and weighting down the ends of the poncho with stones.

Other men made a variety of triangular shelters with groundsheets and stick supports, fixing the ends of the groundsheets with string and short, wooden stakes. A few of the more energetic made shelters from simply woven *atap*, elephant grass, palm leaves or bamboo. Captain Callaghan and

Sergeant Lorrimer, being more experienced in jungle survival, built bamboo rafts and slept on the river, tying the rafts to the base of the tree trunks on the bank. In doing this, they solved the problem of the creepy-crawlies on the ground while also ensuring that the river breeze would keep them cool. For this the other men envied them.

Not too many would have envied Dead-eye. Leaving the relatively open, dry ground near the river bank and heading into the *ulu*, he ran almost immediately into a stretch of *belukar*, or secondary jungle, where the thickets of thorn, bracken and bamboo, almost impenetrable in themselves, were covered with the gargantuan leathery *mengkuang*, the pointed blades of which slashed his face and hands, soaking him in his own blood.

Thirty minutes later, just as the blood was congealing, he sank chest-deep in muddy water and felt the leeches sticking to his legs, hands and body. Continuing to wade through the water, holding his M1 above his head, he temporarily froze when a geometrically patterned snake, the venomous Malay pit viper, emerged from the vegetation by his right elbow, slithered across the branch floating in the water directly in front of him, practically brushing his chest as it crossed his path, then disappeared back into the dense foliage to his left.

Releasing the breath he had been holding in, Dead-eye continued wading and was relieved when the ground beneath his feet turned upwards, letting him rise out of the water as he advanced. Eventually back on marshy land, he moved deeper into the *ulu*, tormented even more now by the many leeches clinging to him and sucking on his blood, but unwilling to stop to remove them, which would have taken too long. Instead, he kept advancing, checking every leaf and branch, only detouring when faced with something hideous in the undergrowth – another snake, a venomous spider, sleeping vampire bats, 10-inch centipedes and nests of hornets whose sting, when not actually fatal, was more painful than being pierced by hot rivets.

Dead-eye braved all of this and stopped only when he suddenly saw the back of a man kneeling on the bank at the other side of a short stretch of leaf-covered swamp water, examining the ground around his bare feet. Though dressed like a Chinese coolie, but with a military cap on his head, he was carrying a British M1 rifle, which marked him as one of Ah Hoi's guerrillas.

Not wanting to fire his own M1 carbine and alert other CT in the area, Dead-eye decided to use his crossbow. Removing it as quietly as possible from where it was strapped across his bergen, he knelt on the grass, cocked the weapon, inserted a lightweight alloy bolt and arrow, then prepared to fire.

At that moment, a large spider, of a species unknown to Dead-eye but about the size of his outspread hand and looking rather like a tarantula, materialized eerily from under the leaves and crawled over his boot. Paralysed with the kind of fear that no human could cause in him, feeling goose pimples all over, his heart suddenly racing, Dead-eye watched as the enormous spider crossed over the toe of his boot, moved up the laces and onto his leg, just above the ankle, then mercifully changed its mind and turned back down, sliding off the other side of the boot and disappearing under the carpet of leaves as eerily as it had first appeared.

Letting his breath out, then sucking in another lungful of air, Dead-eye waited until his racing heart had settled down, then looked at the man across the short stretch of swamp. The man was still kneeling, carefully studying the ground around him.

Dead-eye took aim along the sights of the crossbow, then squeezed the trigger, sending the alloy bolt and arrow racing through the air and straight into the nape of the guerrilla's neck.

The man quivered violently as if whipped, then stood up and turned around to face the river, looking very surprised. He gripped the bolt in his right hand, pulled a little, winced and stopped, then opened and shut his mouth a few times, as if checking if he had feeling left in his neck. He touched the bolt again, winced, shuddered violently, then sank unsteadily to his knees. He tried to pull the bolt out, convulsed in agony, then fell face down in the mud. He shook for a few seconds like an epileptic having a violent fit, then was still.

At that moment, Dead-eye heard a loud rustling in the undergrowth a good distance behind him. Spinning around, he was relieved to see a sweaty Trooper Moffatt blundering like an elephant from the jungle, just south of the route Dead-eye had taken.

Angry at Moffatt's amateurish and noisy advance, Dead-eye was about to wave him down when, to his horror, he saw that an enormous log impregnated with six-inch nails and sharpened hardwood spikes had been suspended above the trail on a rope that formed a trip-wire to release the log. It was, Dead-eye recognized instantly, the hideous booby-trap known as the Chinese Chopper.

'Freeze!' Dead-eye bawled.

Startled, Moffatt froze momentarily, but when he recognized Dead-eye, his evident relief made him forget the warning and he stepped forward again. He tripped over the rope and stumbled a little as the rest of the rope rapidly unravelled and the immense, spiked log fell upon him.

Hearing the noise of snapping branches, Moffatt just had time to glance up before the log smashed down on him, crushing him, piercing him with multiple stab wounds and finally pinning his mangled body to the ground. He hadn't even had time to scream.

'Shit!' Dead-eye whispered, then advanced, crouched low, now checking his surroundings even more carefully, until he reached Moffatt's body. The young trooper had been flattened beneath the log, pressed deeply into the mud. He was covered with an appalling amount of blood and more was squirting out of his numerous wounds.

Dead-eye didn't have to check that Moffatt was dead, but he did look for his weapon, failed to find it, and realized that it must have been buried under him. Knowing that there was little more he could do, Dead-eye headed back the way he had come, not stopping until he reached the camp by the river.

Dead-eye found most of the men asleep in their jungle bashas, with Callaghan and Lorrimer sleeping on bamboo rafts in the middle of the narrow river. Entering the river, which came up to his chest, Dead-eye waded up to Callaghan's raft, shook him awake and told him about the loss of Moffatt.

'If they left that booby-trap,' Captain Callaghan responded pragmatically, 'they've surely left others – and that means the bastards know we're pursuing them. No point in being too careful now. We'll just go in and finish them off. Get a good night's sleep, Trooper.'

'Yes, boss,' Dead-eye said. He waded back to the grassy bank, rolled his bivi-bag out on a soft carpet of leaves, then, no longer concerned about creepy-crawlies, fell into a deep, helpful sleep. When he woke at dawn, he felt older and wiser.

14

When the men moved out the next morning, Dead-eye went on point to lead them through the hellish swamp to where the dead Moffatt was still pinned beneath the fatal log, his body now rendered even more hideous by being covered in bloated flies and red ants.

No one really wanted to touch the bloody, crushed, stabbed corpse but some of the men, at Callaghan's insistence, rolled the log off and buried the trooper in a shallow grave, being forced to beat the flies off as they did so.

Once the body was covered up, the patrol moved on across the short stretch of swamp to where the guerrilla was still lying face down in the mud with the alloy bolt and arrow through his neck, protruding front and rear, the congealed blood around it attracting swarms of flies and an army of ants. More grisly still, some animal from the *ulu* had fed off the corpse, tearing an arm from the shoulder and carrying it off to its lair. The bloody stump of the arm had become an ants' nest being attacked by many different kinds of insects.

'I'm fucked if I'm burying him,' Welsh said. 'Let the animals have him.'

'Why not?' Laughton replied. 'What's left of him will disappear soon enough. Hey, Dead-eye, good shot!'

'Thanks,' Dead-eye said.

'Fucking Robin Hood,' Dennis the Menace said. 'I wouldn't invite that little bastard to a game of darts. You'd be pinned to the fucking board.'

'Do you play darts?' Boney Maronie asked.

'No,' Dead-eye replied. 'I don't drink, so I never go to pubs and have never played darts.'

'Let's all say our thanks,' Boney Maronie said. 'God's still on our side.'

They marched on, deeper into the swamp, leaving the dead guerrilla well behind and keeping their eyes peeled for other booby-traps. In fact, they had only marched another hour when Dead-eye, still on point, saw another Chinese Chopper across the trail. Boney Maronie put it out of action by tearing the rope to shreds with a hail of 9mm bullets from his Owen sub-machine-gun, causing the viciously spiked log to crash to the ground.

'Nice one,' Dennis the Menace said.

An hour later the real nightmare began. First,

they came across a thatch-and-palm lean-to once used by some guerrillas, as could be seen from a pile of ant-covered chicken bones, turtle shells covered in swarms of flies, decaying vegetables and a couple of line drawings showing various routes through the swamp. Excited, Trooper Frank Turner snatched up the maps.

'*Don't touch them!*' Sergeant Lorrimer bellowed – too late. He then threw himself out of the lean-to as a hidden fragmentation grenade, detonated by a trip-wire fixed to the phoney maps, exploded with a deafening roar, hurling Turner backwards in a fountain of loose soil, his flesh shredded by razor-sharp, red-hot shrapnel, and setting fire to the few parts of the lean-to not blown apart.

The scorched, shredded Turner was lying on his back, shuddering spasmodically and screaming like an animal as Lorrimer picked himself up and wiped soil from his face.

'Damn!' he exclaimed, then turned to the other men. 'Don't ever touch anything!' he bawled. 'Check everything first!' He knelt beside the screaming man, saw the scorched and shredded flesh, and was still deciding what to do about him when the man coughed up a mess of blood and phlegm, then shuddered, evacuated his bowels and died.

'Do you want me to call up for a casevac?' Laughton asked.

'What for? He's dead.'

'Just thought you might want the body flown home, Sarge.'

'We'd have to clear an LZ and that would take half the day,' Lorrimer told him, glancing at Callaghan for support and receiving it in the shape of a slight nod. 'Let's bury him here and move on. We're running out of supplies.'

While some of the men were given the unpleasant detail of digging a grave for Turner, Lorrimer took Callaghan aside. 'Do you think D Squadron and the others will be dropped today as agreed?'

'I don't see why not, but I'll get on the blower and check.'

'Can they drop us resups at the same time?'

'I don't think so, Sarge. They're going to need all the space they can get for the men being brought in.'

'My sentiments exactly. And this is our seventh day in this filthy swamp, which means we've run out of half our rations. The men are also running out of patience. I say we wait until we know the others have been dropped, throw a cordon around the swamp, then move in and don't stop until this bloody business is ended, no matter how difficult it is or how bad the casualties.'

'I think you're right,' Callaghan said. 'If we hold back too long, this swamp will do us in before the CT do, so let's go for broke. I'll get on to Major Pryce-Jones and see what he has to say.' Callaghan crossed to where Laughton was kneeling on the swampy ground with his PRC 320 beside him. 'Get me Major Pryce-Jones,' Callaghan said. When Laughton had made contact, Callaghan asked his fellow officer when the drop was going to commence.

'The Kampong Guards of the Malaya Police are on their way right now,' Pryce-Jones replied, 'and I'm just about to head for the airstrip to join the rest of D Squadron. The Kampong Guards are going to block off the coast and we'll be cordoning off the eastern perimeter of the swamp to prevent the CT from getting out that way. We'll work our way into the swamp to link up with you. Have you located them yet? Over.'

'We know they're heading upriver, towards the centre of the swamp and possibly further, so you could make contact before us. Over.'

'OK. We'll send up a flare if we do. You do the same. Good luck, Captain. Over and out.'

The patrol moved on, heading east on a compass bearing, picking an ever more cautious way through the swamp, noses alert for the smell of guerrilla fire smoke or cooking, ears straining through the cacophony of bullfrog croaks for the sound of a human voice, eyes straining in the gloom to see snakes, poisonous spiders, wild boar or more booby-traps. They saw all of those.

Forced to follow the river, they encountered a lot of snakes where they were sheltering in the relative cool of the muddy banks. Most of the snakes slithered away at the sight or sound of booted feet, but some of them were particularly aggressive, rising up in the air and darting forward with their venomous fangs spitting. As it was now clear that the CT knew the British were here – and as their constant use of the *parangs* to hack away the dense foliage was creating a racket anyway – the men were no longer concerned with maintaining silence and either despatched the aggressive snakes with a short burst from their semi-automatic weapons or by slicing through them with the *parangs*. They were often amazed, in the latter case, when the two halves of the bisected reptile wriggled off in separate directions for a considerable distance before finally surrendering to death's stillness.

Welsh had no compunction about breaking the silence when he had to pass under a branch on which was resting an enormous, hairy spider. Pete despatched it – and the branch – with a sustained burst from his Owen.

When an enormous *seladang* virtually exploded out of the undergrowth and charged, bellowing angrily, at some of the men, the wild ox was not stopped by a couple of shots from Dead-eye's M1 carbine, but only by a sustained burst from Lorrimer's more powerful Browning 12-gauge autoloader shotgun. This did not quite lift the huge animal off its feet – as it would have done a man – but it certainly stopped its ferocious advance, made its legs buckle as its intestines slopped out, and finally caused it to sink bloodily to the marshy earth.

Trooper Jimmy Ashman was the first man to see the next Chinese Chopper. Grinning like a schoolkid because he'd seen it before it trapped him, he skirted around it – and tripped over another string stretched along both sides of the narrow track.

His scream was dreadful as he staggered back from the impact of the spear that was suddenly thrusting out of his chest. It had been fired from a bow concealed in the earth and operated by a trigger mechanism set off by the hidden trip-cord. Ashman kept screaming as he dropped his M1, staggering backwards as if punch-drunk, and instinctively tried to jerk the spear out of his smashed chest and pierced heart. He was dying even as he was attempting this and dead by the time he fell backwards into a pool of mud.

Welsh automatically sub-machine-gunned the

activating cords of the booby-trap, then also pep-
pered the area on both sides of the track, just to
be sure. When they knew the ground was safe, the
men dug a shallow grave for Ashman, buried him,
conducted a simple ceremony and then continued
their march.

About an hour later, when they had managed
to hack their way through another 500 yards
of murderously dense secondary jungle, Lorrimer
and Dead-eye, sharing point duty together, spotted
three guerrillas about 50 yards away across a
stretch of open, rust-brown water.

After using a hand signal to tell the rest of the
squadron to drop to the ground, Lorrimer indicated
that Dead-eye should follow him. He discarded his
bergen and other kit, slipped into the water, holding
his Browning shotgun above his head, waited for
Dead-eye to follow suit, then grabbed a floating
log. With the log in front of them, they both
inched through the water, resting their weapons
near the top of the log, though slightly behind it,
so that only the log would have been seen if the
guerrillas had turned around. When they neared
the other side of the stretch of open water, both
still hidden by the log and about 50 yards from
the bank, they saw that the guerrillas were two
men and a woman.

As they were quietly bringing their weapons up

into the firing position, resting the barrels on the floating log, they heard the distant rumble of aircraft and saw the guerrillas pointing at the sky.

A Beverley was flying overhead. Even as they all looked up, four separate sticks of men dropped out in different directions – from the port and starboard doors; left and right of the boom door – and their parachutes billowed out, one after the other, to let them descend silently onto the eastern side of the swamp. Though neither Lorrimer nor Dead-eye said a word, they both knew the men descending on the parachutes were the Kampong Guards, to be followed shortly by SAS D Squadron.

Lorrimer nodded at Dead-eye, then aimed along the upraised sights of his Browning shotgun. Dead-eye did the same with his M1 carbine. They opened fire simultaneously, taking out the two men, who convulsed in a dramatic explosion of spitting soil and foliage. The woman, however, jumped to her feet and fled into the jungle.

'Damn!' Lorrimer exclaimed. 'Let's go get her!' Pushing the log aside, they both waded to the bank, scrambled out, dripping wet, and raced into the jungle after the woman. She disappeared like a wisp of smoke, as if she had never been. 'Damn!' Lorrimer said again. Returning to the stretch of water, they checked the dead guerrillas, found nothing of importance on them, so slipped back into the water and waded back to the other side, holding their weapons above their heads. As they were scrambling up the far bank, a second Beverley flew overhead, disgorging another group of paratroopers to the east.

'D Squadron,' Lorrimer said.

'Good,' Dead-eye replied. 'We'll soon have the CT boxed in, then this'll be over in no time.'

'I wouldn't count on it,' Lorrimer warned.

They then hacked their way through the dense foliage, back to the main party.

By the following morning, the Kampong Guards had laid barbed wire along the coast, thus blocking all entrances to the area from the east. Simultaneously, D Squadron had tightened the cordon around the guerrillas by moving to a point on the River Tengi several miles upstream from Callaghan's group. The two groups were now closing towards one another in a pincer movement around the CT. Even more effectively, the Kampong Police, with the aid of Royal Marine Commandos, also threw a huge cordon around the whole swamp perimeter and arranged for helicopters to fly over the area, scanning the open spaces in the watery swamp for signs of Ah Hoi and his guerrillas.

It was now fifteen days since the SAS had dropped into the swamp and all the men were suffering from prickly heat and a variety of infections. Many had legs and arms ripped by thorns, with the wounds infected and badly ulcerated. Nevertheless, when Major Pryce-Jones contacted Captain Callaghan to inform him that the rest of D Squadron, under his command, was presently marching from the eastern perimeter into the swamp, Callaghan pressed his men on for the final push against the CT.

As they neared the centre of the swamp, they had to watch out for an increasing number of booby-traps, as well as actual guerrillas. The latter suddenly started appearing in the undergrowth just long enough to fire quick bursts from their assault rifles or tommy-guns before disappearing again. When this happened, the SAS troopers broke from their lengthy single file and instead fanned out across the *ulu* to form a broad cordon composed of two- or four-man teams, from which the CT could not escape.

Aware that they were now hedged in on all sides, the CT responded by attempting a suicidal last-ditch stand.

Captain Callaghan stuck close to Trooper

Laughton, who had the PRC 320, through which he kept in regular contact with Major Pryce-Jones as the latter advanced into the swamp from the east.

When the first CT jumped up from behind some foliage just ahead, firing his tommy-gun and wounding one SAS trooper, Callaghan sent up a flare. The CT sniper disappeared as quickly as he had materialized, but Dead-eye switched to the M203 grenade-launcher on his M1 and fired a 40mm shell where the guerrilla had been, blowing the foliage to pieces and setting fire to the bark of a tree. When the smoke cleared, the sniper's scorched, shredded body was revealed, sprawled brokenly over a fallen tree trunk.

'Advance!' Sergeant Lorrimer bawled, then jumped up and ran, leaping over the dead guerrilla and rushing into the jungle, though safely at the half-crouch, with Dead-eye coming up close behind him. When another guerrilla appeared, taking aim with a Belgian FN assault rifle, Lorrimer fired his Browning shotgun from the hip, three shots in quick succession, and the guerrilla was picked up and punched back into the shrubbery with half of his chin gone, his throat a bloody mess and the bones of his chest exposed through the gashes in his tunic.

He had hardly hit the ground when two more

guerrillas jumped up, to be despatched by a fusillade from Dead-eye's deadly accurate M1 carbine. Dead-eye then switched again to the grenade-launcher, firing on a trajectory that landed the grenade just beyond the men he had killed. The explosion was catastrophic – more than the grenade warranted – and he realized even before the flames had flickered out and the smoke had dispersed that he had set off another booby-trap, probably some kind of land-mine.

'Booby-traps!' he bawled. His warning, however, was too late for one trooper, who dived for the cover of a small sapling, shaking it enough to dislodge the mortar shell lodged loosely in its branches. Dead-eye saw it falling and threw himself to the ground just in time to avoid the deafening blast of the explosion. When the showering debris had settled down, he looked to the side and saw a severed leg pumping blood onto the green grass only yards away. Jumping back to his feet, he saw the rest of the trooper, a leg here, an arm there. Realizing that nothing could be done, he raced on, attempting to catch up with Lorrimer, who was directly ahead, with Dennis the Menace and Boney Maronie directly behind him, and a grim-faced Welsh bringing up the rear.

By now the jungle was filled with smoke and

reeking of cordite, reverberating with the sounds of explosions and the screams of wounded or dying men. Dropping to one knee to replace his empty magazine, Dead-eye almost choked on the smoke. He wiped tears from his eyes, then saw an SAS trooper tripping over a hidden rope, thus releasing a springing shaft with a wooden spear lashed to its tip. Impaled through the stomach, the soldier was punched violently backwards. He stared down in shock at the spear, almost collapsed, but was held up by the springing shaft. He screamed in agony, then died there on his feet. He remained that way, held upright even in death, as Dead-eye jumped up and advanced again into the smouldering, smoke-wreathed *ulu*.

Dennis the Menace and Boney Maronie, working as a team, were advancing at the half-crouch just ahead of Dead-eye when they saw another guerrilla pop up from behind some undergrowth to take a shot at them. They dropped to the ground and the bullets whistled over their heads, but a second burst kicked up a line of spitting soil between them, making them roll apart.

The ground caved in under Boney and he disappeared from view, then let forth a dreadful, anguished scream.

Shocked, Dennis the Menace released the pin on a fragmentation grenade and hurled it towards the guerrillas. He covered his ears while it exploded, sending foliage and loose soil geysering skyward, then wriggled across to where Boney Maronie had disappeared and was still screaming dreadfully. Finding a hole in the ground – previously covered by a false surface raised on breakable supports – he looked down to see his friend writhing on a bed of wooden stakes that had been sharpened and then smeared with excrement to cause maximum damage.

'Punji pit!' Dennis bawled like a madman. 'Help! For God's sake!'

Callaghan and Laughton appeared out of swirling smoke to kneel beside Dennis the Menace and look down into the pit.

'Dear God!' Callaghan exclaimed softly while Laughton winced.

Welsh dropped down beside them and also looked into the punji pit, where Boney Maronie was still writhing and screaming. 'Fucking hell!' Welsh groaned. 'What a way to go!'

Outraged, Dennis the Menace dived at Welsh, but was hauled back by Captain Callaghan. 'What the hell do you think you're doing, Trooper?'

'He said . . .'

'Never mind, damn it,' Callaghan interjected sharply. 'Let's get that man out of there.'

'How?' Laughton asked.

Sergeant Lorrimer and Dead-eye emerged from the swirling smoke and dropped to their knees beside Captain Callaghan.

'Cover us,' Callaghan said. 'We've got to get Boney out of that pit, so I'm going down into it. Make sure no one gets near us.'

'Right, boss,' Sergeant Lorrimer replied, then pointed his index finger at Laughton. 'Lay down covering fire with that Bren gun,' he said, 'and keep firing until we tell you to stop.'

'Will do,' Laughton said, unstrapping the Bren gun from his bergen, releasing the tripod, mounting the gun and aiming along the sights at the undergrowth straight ahead. When he saw the undergrowth shifting, he opened fire and kept firing, the gun making a sustained roaring sound. Lorrimer did the same with his Browning shotgun, blasting the foliage to shreds, and Dead-eye fired one shot after the other, his hawk eyes picking out every movement of foliage and never failing to find the guerrilla causing it.

'Keep it up!' Callaghan bawled over the din as he dropped his bergen and webbing to the muddy ground. Freed of all encumbrances, he lay belly-down on the grass, slithered backwards, and very carefully lowered himself into the punji pit, where Boney Maronie was still pinioned on the excrement-smeared wooden stakes. Boney had stopped moving to prevent further injury and anguish, and was breathing heavily while staring up at Callaghan with terrified eyes.

Callaghan carefully placed his feet between the stakes, steadied himself, then leant over Boney.

Pain and fear had made the trooper almost unrecognizable. Blood was pouring profusely from the many wounds in his back and legs. He was doomed, but he still had to be rescued.

'Captain . . .' he managed to croak, then sucked in some more air.

'This is going to hurt terribly,' Callaghan said, 'but you'll just have to endure it.'

'Yes, Cap'n. Oh, God!'

A mortar shell exploded near the men above, causing loose soil and foliage to rain down over Callaghan's head and Boney Maronie's sweating, frightened face. When the debris finally settled, Callaghan checked that the men above were still firing their weapons – obviously unhurt, they were – then took a deep breath, leaned over Boney Maronie, and said: 'OK, bite your lower lip. This'll hurt like hell.'

He took hold of Boney Maronie's shoulders and eased him up off the sharpened stakes. When Boney Maronie started screaming, Callaghan stopped being gentle and hauled him upright as fast as he could. Boney Maronie screamed even louder, his body quivering like a bowstring. When he was free of the stakes he collapsed into Callaghan's embrace and clung sobbing to him.

'It's not over yet,' Callaghan said, 'and you can't let me down. Scream as much as you want, lad.' He glanced directly above him. Welsh was looking down. The others were continuing to pour gunfire into the jungle where the guerrillas were lurking. 'OK, Welsh,' Callaghan said. 'You've got to haul Boney Maronie up. It doesn't matter how much it hurts him, nor how much he screams – you've just got to do it.' Still holding Boney Maronie in his arms, he repeated: 'You scream as much as you want, lad. But try to climb out of here. OK, let's do it.'

Callaghan released Boney Maronie and patted him on the cheek. Boney just stood there, his feet between the stakes, swaying, a dazed look in his eyes, his back and legs pouring blood.

'Yes, boss,' he managed to croak.

'Raise your hands as high as you can,' Callaghan said. Boney did as he was told. Welsh grabbed his hands, glanced at Captain Callaghan, received his nod and started pulling Boney Maronie up. Boney screamed like an animal, being torn apart by pain, but Callaghan pushed as Pete Welsh pulled . . . and eventually Boney was out of the pit, face down on the ground.

Though no longer screaming, he was sobbing like a child, helplessly, shamelessly, hardly aware of himself. Captain Callaghan leaned forward, stroked the back of his head, and said, 'We've got to leave you for now, Boney. We can't casevac you yet. We'll call in a chopper just as soon as this is over, but in the meantime you'll just have to endure it. There's no more we can do.'

'The pain,' Boney groaned. 'God, the pain.'

'I'm going to give you some morphine,' Callaghan said. 'That's all I can do for now.'

'Yes, boss. Jesus, yes!'

The number and depth of the wounds, combined with the excrement left in them from the stakes, convinced Callaghan that Boney could not survive. Nevertheless, he put him out of his pain by injecting him with morphine, smeared the areas between the wounds with river mud, which would help to keep away the insects, and finally covered him with a waterproof poncho that would help to keep his temperature even.

'Right,' he said, speaking loudly against the roaring of the combined weapons of Lorrimer, Dead-eye, Laughton and Dennis the Menace. 'That's all I can do. We have to go on now.'

'No, boss,' Boney managed to say, still being face down in the grass because he couldn't possibly lie on his badly wounded back. 'The guerrillas might pass through here. Please, God, boss, you know what . . .'

He didn't have to say more. Callaghan removed his own 9mm Browning High Power handgun from its holster and laid it on the grass by Boney's fingers, to enable him to join the 'Exit Club', should the guerrillas find him still alive.

'OK, Boney, good luck.'

Dennis the Menace stopped firing and turned around. 'We just leave him?' he asked, sounding choked.

'We've no choice,' Callaghan said. 'Now get up and advance to the east and don't look back, Trooper.'

'Yes, boss,' Dennis the Menace said. He turned away to hide his tears and said, 'OK, Dead-eye, are you all set?'

'Yes,' Dead-eye said, sounding as cool as a block of ice. 'Let's put an end to this shit.' He stood up, switched his M1 to the grenade-launcher, inserted a 40mm shell, then fired it at the undergrowth straight ahead. When the shell exploded, tearing the foliage apart, setting some of it on fire, and filling the area with smoke, he and the others raced on at the half-crouch, leaving Boney Maronie to his fate.

Dennis the Menace, determined not to show his tears, was racing out ahead, though still a good way behind Welsh.

When a flare exploded over the *ulu* to the east, indicating that the rest of D Squadron had made contact with the CT, the men knew they were close to the guerrillas' camp.

Welsh saw his chance then. Consumed with the rage that had fuelled most of his life, landing him in trouble time after time, but making him a good soldier if not a good SAS trooper, he wanted to wreak his revenge on Dennis the Menace.

He didn't care what chances he took to do it – he just had to do it – so he raced on ahead, taking point, but suicidally, crashing through the undergrowth, firing his sub-machine-gun from the hip, lobbing hand-grenades at anything that moved, and running into the blinding smoke like a man both invisible and invincible. He managed to kill quite a few of the guerrillas, but no one touched him.

Eventually arriving at a trampled track that sloped downhill into a low, sheltered area, Welsh suspected that the CT might be down there, preparing to make their last stand. Knowing from experience that sloping ground was the ideal place for a spike trap – where man or beast would step down harder than normal, thus making the false surface cave in – he carefully checked the track, convinced that it would be booby-trapped, and did indeed find the false surface of a spike trap, covered with loose soil and leaves.

Stepping carefully around it, he deliberately knelt on the ground at the other side, facing downhill.

Dennis the Menace was the first to emerge from the smoke-wreathed forest at the top of the gentle rise. When he saw Welsh, he stopped, glanced left and right, then waited for the nod indicating 'Advance'. When he received it, he advanced at the half-crouch down the hill, not seeing the spike trap.

Welsh smiled grimly as Dennis the Menace hurried down the slope and approached the murderous spike trap.

Just before he reached the trap, however, a guerrilla stepped out from the trees behind him and took aim with a British tommy-gun.

Without even thinking, Welsh opened fire with his Owen, swinging it in an arc, cutting across the guerrilla, throwing him into convulsions, practically lifting him off his feet and hurling him backwards into the undergrowth.

Dennis the Menace froze, glanced back over his shoulder, then turned to the front again as Welsh, hardly believing that he was hearing his own voice, bawled: 'Spike trap! Get off the track! Come down through the undergrowth!' As Dennis the Menace did just that, the others emerged from the jungle behind him and Welsh shouted out the same warning. When they had all passed the spike trap and were looking downhill, Captain Callaghan patted Welsh on the shoulder, saying: 'Good man. Now are those commie bastards down there or not?'

'I think they're down there,' Welsh said quietly.

'Then let's go and get them.'

They advanced down the hill and reached a stretch of sheltered flatland that ended back at the bank of the curving river.

The CTs had moved on.

15

The woman emerged from the trees and stood at the far side of the river, ghostly in the cold morning mist. It was just after first light. Having been on guard duty all night, Dead-eye was dog-tired and thought he was seeing things, but soon realized that the woman was real enough. She was tiny, emaciated, wearing an olive-green uniform, standing in bare feet, with her black hair pulled up and tied in a pony tail at the back of her head.

Having emerged from the *ulu*, she stood for a moment on the far bank and looked directly at Dead-eye. He was aiming his M1 carbine at her from behind the wall of loose branches and leaves he had built as a jungle variation on the normal loose-stoned sangar. Seemingly unconcerned that Dead-eye might fire at her, the woman stepped down into the river, then waded across, clambered out the other side and walked right up to him.

Only about 4 feet 6 inches tall, she was practically skeletal and suffering from beri-beri, with a visible puffiness around her knees, ankles and wrists. But she must have once been pretty.

'My name is Ah Niet,' she said. 'I come with a message from Ah Hoi. Take me to your leader.'

Climbing to his feet, Dead-eye crossed a few yards of grass to shake Dennis the Menace awake. 'Come on, Dennis, wake up!' When Dennis had rubbed his eyes and was looking reasonably alert, Dead-eye pointed backwards to the tiny female guerrilla, saying: 'We've got a visitor. She's come from Ah Hoi with a message. I'm going to take her to Callaghan, so take over my guard duty.'

Dennis the Menace looked in surprise at the short, wasted Chinese woman, rubbed his eyes again, then picked up his M1 carbine and climbed to his feet. 'Surprise, surprise,' he said. 'She looks like she hasn't eaten a good meal in months.'

'She probably hasn't,' Dead-eye said. 'Take over my sangar.'

'Right,' Dennis the Menace said and walked back to the branch-and-palm sangar, where the woman was patiently waiting for him.

'She speaks English?' Dennis the Menace asked.

'Yes,' Dead-eye said.

'A little,' the woman corrected him.

'That's enough. Come with me.' As Dennis

settled into Dead-eye's thatched sangar, the latter led Ah Niet across the clearing, through the trees and back to another part of the river bank, where Captain Callaghan was wisely sleeping on his floating bamboo raft tethered to some branches. When Dead-eye called out to him, he opened his eyes. Seeing the woman, he used the rope to pull the raft to the bank, then clambered on to the grassy verge. He studied the woman thoughtfully.

'This lady is called Ah Niet,' Dead-eye said. 'She claims to be a messenger from Ah Hoi.'

'Is this true?' Callaghan asked.

'Yes, sir,' Ah Niet replied.

'Where's Ah Hoi now?'

The woman waved her hand vaguely in the direction of the jungle on the other side of the river. 'Over there. Deeper in *ulu*. Near heart of swamp. It hard for you there.'

'I'm sure,' Callaghan replied smoothly. 'So what's the message?'

'Ah Hoi is willing to come out of swamp if you give compensation. For each of his men. Also amnesty for those now in prison.'

'Compensation? Do you mean money?'

'Yes, sir. A sum to be kindly agreed between us.'

'Wait here,' Callaghan said. 'Dead-eye, give her

something to eat and drink. Your emergency rations will do.'

'That's *my* rations we're talking about, boss.'

'I'm a generous man with other men's scran. Now I'm off to talk to Major Pryce-Jones on Trooper Laughton's radio. I'll be back in a minute.'

While Callaghan was away, talking to Pryce-Jones on the PRC 320, Dead-eye told the clearly exhausted Ah Niet to rest on the grass. When she was sitting at his feet, he knelt beside her, gave her some chocolate from his escape belt, then poured water from his bottle into a tin mug and handed it to her. She wolfed the chocolate down and drank the water greedily, confirming that she had gone hungry for some time. A few minutes later, Callaghan returned, now accompanied by a sleepy Lorrimer.

'No deal,' Callaghan said when the woman stood to face him. 'No money, no amnesty. Tell Ah Hoi he's surrounded. The whole swamp has been encircled by Kampong Guards and another squadron of SAS troopers is moving in on your encampment from the east, to form a cordon completed by this group. Your leader has a choice between surrendering within twelve hours or death in the swamp. If our foot soldiers fail in this task, the RAF will bomb him out of hiding. That's the message you're taking back.'

'Yes, sir.' Ah Niet pointed to the south. 'Paddy-field over there. If Ah Hoi comes out, he surrenders in paddy-field. Thank you, sir. I say goodbye.'

She waded back across the river, then dissolved into the *ulu* like a ghost.

'Alert the men,' Callaghan said. 'We're going to move out and set up our camp in that paddy-field. Let's pray he comes out.'

After being wakened, the men were allowed to wash in the river and have a breakfast of high-calorie rations. When ready, they demolished their wide variety of jungle shelters, shook out and rolled up their ponchos, packed their bergens, strapped them to their backs, then picked up their personal weapons and moved out one by one, first wading across the river, holding their weapons above their heads, then falling into a single file that snaked through the *ulu*, heading south towards the distant paddy-field.

It was not a long journey in terms of distance – only two miles – but that part of the *ulu*, being near the swamp's centre, was a vile combination of swamp and murderously dense *belukar*. The swamp water, which usually came up to the men's chests, was filled with snakes, leeches, floating logs and broken, obstructive branches. Its brown, moss-covered surface was covered constantly with swarms of noisily buzzing flies, midges, whining mosquitoes and hornets whose stings were agonizing. Before long, some of the men had eyes so swollen from mosquito bites that they could hardly see.

When not being tormented in the chest-deep water, the men were faced with the dreaded *belukar*, which, with its thick, tangled *mengkuang* grass and razor-sharp giant leaves, had to be hacked away with *parangs* and sometimes even uprooted by hand. The first mile took the men almost four hours of unremitting labour and when eventually they were allowed to stop for a rest, they were kept busy removing the bloodsucking leeches from their bruised skin, either by burning them off with cigarettes or by sprinkling them with salt and then pulling them off. Both ways left them a tremendous number of cuts and scars, many of which were already suppurating.

Having removed the leeches, the troopers then had to plunge back into the water, where they were attacked all over again. Emerging from the water about half an hour later, again covered in leeches, they had to hack their way through another long stretch of *belukar*, which left them exhausted and bathed in sweat. By last light, when they were emerging from the swamp to the wide, relatively cool paddy-field, most of them had lost pounds in weight and were looking as bad as they felt.

Mercifully, they could rest while waiting to see whether or not Ah Hoi would emerge with his guerrillas before the twelve-hour deadline was up. Constructing another wide variety of shelters around the edge of the dry paddy-field, the men settled in gratefully, some even managing to sleep, but most of them just resting until they were called for guard duty or to go out on point.

At dusk, a few hours before the deadline, the lights of many torches appeared in the *ulu* at the far side of the paddy-field, weaving to and fro like stars in the night sky as a large group advanced. Captain Callaghan immediately ordered his men out of their shelters, then formed them into a defensive cordon along their side of the paddy-field, with the field covered by tripod-mounted Bren guns and personal weapons.

The guerrillas, men and women, emerged from the jungle with their weapons strapped across their backs, one hand raised in a sign of surrender, the other holding a torchlight.

The woman, Ah Niet, was at the head of the group, beside a short, tubby man wearing a grey jacket with high collar, grey trousers, a military cap and a pair of *terumpas*, the wooden clog held on by rubber straps.

'That must be Ah Hoi,' Callaghan whispered to Lorrimer.

271

'Let's hope so, boss.'

The man was, in fact, Ah Hoi, and introduced himself thus when he and Callaghan met in the middle of the paddy-field. When Callaghan saluted him, Ah Hoi simply nodded by way of response. He was short, fat and rather arrogant, but nothing about him suggested the kind of man who could personally disembowel a woman in her eighth month of pregnancy.

'This is not a surrender,' he said, speaking Mandarin, which Callaghan understood. 'I am simply avoiding the senseless slaughter of my honourable forces. We will win in the end.'

'Ask your men to hand over their weapons,' Captain Callaghan replied, ignoring Ah Hoi's humourless propaganda.

'Of course,' Ah Hoi said with a wintry smile. When he nodded at his men, not saying a word, they unstrapped their weapons, removed them from their backs, and reverentially laid them on the dry paddy-field. At a command from Lorrimer, some of the SAS men started picking up the weapons while ordering the unarmed guerrillas to squat on the ground.

Callaghan, meanwhile, was using Laughton's radio to contact Major Pryce-Jones, presently still moving in from the east with D Squadron. After being informed of Ah Hoi's surrender, Pryce-Jones promised to send over some helicopters to lift off the guerrillas and transfer them to the camp in Johore.

When Callaghan had finished speaking to Pryce-Jones, he ordered flares to be set off to mark the paddy-field as the LZ for the choppers. When this had been done, he turned back to Ah Hoi, who had remained standing, as still as a statue, beside the diminutive Ah Niet.

'Are all your men here?' Callaghan asked.

'No,' Ah Hoi replied. 'Another group is located at another camp, deeper in the jungle. As they have no radios, we could not communicate, but Ah Niet will take you to them and help you bring them back out.'

'She doesn't look fit enough to survive another journey into the swamp.'

'She will do as ordered.'

'Good,' Callaghan said. In fact, being already drained of blood by the leeches and covered in the sores they had inflicted, he dreaded going back into the swamp. Nevertheless, it had to be done, so when a combination of RAF and Army Air Corps Whirlwind, Dragonfly and Sycamore helicopters had started lifting the guerrillas, including Ah Hoi, off the paddy-field, he let his own men rest while he returned to the swamp with Ah Niet, Lorrimer, Dead-eye and Dennis the Menace.

This final hike was hellish.

It soon became clear to Callaghan and the others that Ah Niet had been seriously weakened by the beri-beri and was having considerable trouble in breathing, let alone guiding them through the swamp, which consisted, in this area, mostly of muddy water covered in white pollen and green moss. It was also filled with drifting logs, thorny branches and cutting leaves, as well as being covered with the usual swarms of noisy, aggressive insects. Water snakes, many venomous, glided by just under the surface too often for comfort. Even more debilitating was the fact that the group was forced to virtually swim most of the way, the men holding their weapons above their heads. This caused cramp, other darting, distracting pains and general exhaustion.

Though clearly very ill, Ah Niet led the way, swimming in total silence, but stopping frequently to get her breath back. She vomited three times and coughed up blood twice, yet when Callaghan asked her if she wanted to turn back, she shook her head and said they had to go on as Ah Hoi had ordered.

'Such devotion!' Lorrimer whispered.

'Yeah,' Dennis the Menace replied. 'Makes you want to puke, don't it?'

Finally, as they were approaching what Ah Niet

claimed was the location of the other guerrillas, her strength gave out completely, she had a dreadful coughing fit, bringing up blood and phlegm, and then, before anyone could catch her, splashed face first into the water, sank beneath the surface, and was carried away under some drifting foliage. When she surfaced, about 20 yards away, she was no longer breathing.

'Fucking hell,' Dennis the Menace said. '*Now* what do we do?'

'We leave her here,' Captain Callaghan said pragmatically. 'There's nothing else we *can* do. Our job is to find the rest of the guerrillas and bring them out of the swamp. According to Ah Niet, they're somewhere around here, so let's go and find them.'

'If we go without Ah Niet,' Dead-eye said, 'we might not be welcome.'

'We'll know soon enough,' Callaghan said.

Indeed, they had walked only a few yards after clambering out of the swamp when the jungle exploded with the roaring of the guerrilla's rifles and tommy-guns. Up at the front on point, Dennis the Menace took the brunt of the fire, performing a St Vitus dance in the middle of a violent convulsion of exploding foliage, then falling backwards into prickly shrubbery, pumping blood from a great many bullet wounds.

As Dennis the Menace was dying, Lorrimer was retreating backwards the way they had just come, firing his Browning shotgun from the hip at the guerrillas he saw perched in the trees. Branches and leaves were blown apart, almost as if dynamited, and some guerrillas screamed and plunged to the ground in a noisy shower of foliage.

Dead-eye, meanwhile, had run to Dennis the Menace, where he lay on his back across some bushes, curved like a bow, but with most of his insides turned out by a hail of bullets. Discovering that his friend was dead, Dead-eye was filled with cold rage and advanced fearlessly on the guerrillas, firing his M1 carbine at anything that moved. He then switched to the M203 grenade-launcher, tearing a line of jungle to shreds with a series of fragmentation grenades, all aimed with devastating accuracy.

Even as the wounded guerrillas were screaming in agony, and while smoke and flames were curling in bright-yellow and blue tendrils through the dark-green foliage, now curtained in black smoke, Dead-eye was fixing his bayonet to the barrel of his M1 and preparing to engage in hand-to-hand combat, which would have been suicidal.

Luckily, he was stopped from doing so by Callaghan, who pulled him back, bawling: 'Don't be a damned fool! We've got to return to the paddy-field and call in the RAF. Come on, Dead-eye, let's go!'

'No, damn it!'

'*Let's go!*'

Even as Callaghan was pulling Dead-eye back to the bank of the river running through the swamp, Lorrimer was being attacked by a female guerrilla swinging a *parang*. Momentarily startled to see a woman in front of him, Lorrimer was slower than usual in getting off a shot from his Browning, thus giving her time to swing her *parang* in a horizontal sweep, lopping off his head as precisely as if it had been guillotined.

The head flew through the air, spewing blood in its wake, and landed on the marshy ground a few feet from where Callaghan and Dead-eye were making their retreat, firing on the move.

When Dead-eye saw the severed head, he thought he was hallucinating. It was the right way up, resting on a neck that was pouring blood into the grass. Even more ghoulish and terrifying, Lorrimer's eyes were actually moving in their sockets, first left, then right, but eventually turning up to focus on Dead-eye in an oddly pleading, demented, then dazed manner. Just as Dead-eye understood what he was actually seeing, the eyes in the severed head rolled in their sockets, then froze in the finality of death.

Dead-eye let out a low, gargling sound, then went cold all over.

'Let's go!' Callaghan snapped, ignoring the severed head and tugging Dead-eye towards the river bank. When Dead-eye failed to move, Callaghan brutally slapped his face and snapped: 'Come on, damn it!'

Jerked free from his shocked reverie, Dead-eye turned away from the river, dropped to one knee, then again switched on the M203 grenade-launcher and began to inflict as much damage as humanly possible on the jungle within his line of vision. While Callaghan looked on, not daring to stop him, Dead-eye used up his whole supply of grenades, causing dreadful devastation, fire and smoke and much screaming. When he had run out of grenades, he switched back to the rifle mode and repeated the same, coldly methodical performance, emptying one magazine, changing it for another, emptying that and changing again until nothing was left. He then stood up, stared coldly at Callaghan, and said in a hoarse, emotionless whisper: 'OK, boss, it's done. Let's get the hell out of here.'

Both men plunged back into the swamp and, mostly wading, but sometimes actually swimming, defying the river snakes and ignoring the swarming insects, made their way back to the moonlit paddy-field. There, the last of the guerrillas had been lifted off and the evacuation of the SAS troops was beginning.

'I want that man to have priority,' Callaghan said, pointing at Dead-eye. 'Get him back to Johore and let him sleep until he awakens. I want him looked after.'

'Yes, boss,' Lieutenant Ralph Ellis said. 'Hear you loud and clear, boss.' The pilot helped Dead-eye into his Sikorski S-55 Whirlwind, then flew him back to Johore.

Twenty-four hours later, the few guerrillas remaining in the *ulu* emerged to surrender.

16

Once the remaining CTs had emerged from the swamp, a group of SAS troopers went back in to recover the body of Dennis the Menace and the severed head and body of Sergeant Lorrimer.

Simultaneously, another group retraced their own footsteps to pick up Boney Maronie, dead or alive. In fact, he was dead. He had not been forced to join the 'Exit Club' – committing suicide to prevent himself from falling into the hands of the enemy – but had bled to death from the many wounds inflicted on him by the punji pit.

His body, along with those of the others, was shipped back to England for proper burial.

The surrender of the Communist Terrorists in the Telok Anson swamp marked the beginning of the end of the Emergency in Malaya. Shortly after being taken into captivity, Ah Hoi was given the choice between prison or exile in China. Choosing the latter, he was flown out of Malaya. When he had gone, the SAS, no longer needing to fight in the jungle, concentrated on the hearts-and-minds campaign, proving once and for all that they had a long-term future as a regiment with unusual capabilities, ranging from the military to the diplomatic.

Once back in Britain, Major Pryce-Jones and Captain Callaghan set about the creation of the Selection and Training programme they had discussed at great length in Malaya. By 1960 when the Regiment was transferred from Merebrook Camp, Malvern, Worcestershire, to what would become its permanent home at Bradbury Lines, Redhill, Hereford, the 'bad apples' had been weeded out and the more stringent mental and physical tests applied to all new applicants, ensuring that they were the *crème de la crème* of the military services.

Pete Welsh and Alf Laughton, formerly considered 'bad apples' but having proved themselves in Malaya, actually survived the weeding-out process for the revitalized SAS and went on to become reliable NCOs. The former lost his life in Borneo in 1964; the latter survived that same campaign and returned to Bradbury Lines to become a ruthlessly efficient member of the Directing Staff (DT) at 22 SAS Training Wing, Hereford.

Major Pryce-Jones was RTU'd to the Scots

Guards, but eventually returned to the SAS as a Commanding Officer at Stirling Lines, Hereford, retiring shortly after his successful involvement in the Falklands War of 1982.

Captain Callaghan, promoted to Major shortly after the Regiment transferred to Bradbury Lines, Hereford, went on to lead D Squadron during the Borneo campaign of 1964, where the former 'troublemakers', Pete Welsh and Alf Laughton, both served well under him.

Trooper Richard 'Dead-eye Dick' Parker was psychologically scarred for all time by his experiences in the Telok Anson swamp, yet was, also, oddly enhanced by them. Though haunted by the deaths of Dennis the Menace and Boney Maronie, as well as suffering repeated nightmares about the severed head of Sergeant Lorrimer – whom he had respected so much, almost like a father figure – he soon realized that he had never been happier than when in Malaya and was, for better or worse, a natural soldier.

Apart from being in the SAS, he had no interest in life.

This was proven in 1961 when, after three years of monumental boredom with a peacetime fighting force, he married a girl he had met in Hereford, had a few good months in bed with her, then realized that they had nothing to say to one another when they were not actually making love. By 1963, when Dead-eye was posted with the squadron to Borneo, the marriage was over.

Having seen so many die, mostly those whom he respected, Dead-eye, when he returned from Borneo in 1966, stopped socializing and spent most of his spare time alone, reading books on military theory. He was a man who loved war and understood at the same time that what he most loved would inevitably kill those he loved the most. He therefore decided to protect himself from that kind of pain. His isolation protected him.

By 1972, when Dead-eye was serving in Oman, in the Arabian Gulf, he had become one of the most private, feared and respected members of the SAS. This was appropriate, for by that time the SAS had become the most private, feared and respected body of fighting men in the world.

Dead-eye, an island unto himself, was proud to be part of it.

... continued from front of book

All at £4.99